SOCIETY AND POLITICS
in Ancient Rome

ESSAYS AND SKETCHES

SOCIETY AND POLITICS
in Ancient Rome

ESSAYS AND SKETCHES

By

Frank Frost Abbott

BIBLO AND TANNEN
New York
1963

BIBLO and TANNEN
BOOKSELLERS and PUBLISHERS, Inc.
63 Fourth Avenue New York 3, N. Y.

Library of Congress Catalog Card Number: 63-10767

Printed in U.S.A. by
NOBLE OFFSET PRINTERS, INC.
NEW YORK 3, N. Y.

To

M. A. P.

PREFATORY NOTE

THE papers which are included in this volume have been written at intervals during the last ten or fifteen years. Two of them, "Literature and the Common People of Rome" and "Roman Women in the Trades and the Professions," are now published for the first time. The others have appeared in the *Transactions of the American Philological Association*, the *Arena*, the *Classical Journal*, *Classical Philology*, *Modern Philology*, the *New England Magazine*, the *Sewanee Review*, *Scribner's Magazine*, and the *Yale Review*, and to the publishers of these periodicals the writer is indebted for permission to reproduce them here. The social, political, and literary questions which are discussed in them—the participation of women in public life, municipal politics, the tendencies of parliamentary government, realism in fiction, the influence of the theatre, and like matters—were not peculiar to Roman civilization, but they are of all time, and confront all civilized peoples. We are grappling with them to-day, and to see what form they took at another time and what solutions of them or attempts at solving them another highly civilized people made may not be without profit or interest to us. The common inheritance of difficult problems which we thus share with the Romans has led the writer to compare ancient and modern conditions in some detail, or to contrast them, as the case may be. In fact, most of the papers are in some measure comparative studies of certain phases of life at Rome and in our own day. It is hoped, therefore, that the book will be of some interest to the general reader as well as to the special student of Roman life and literature.

FRANK FROST ABBOTT.

PRINCETON, *June 2*, 1909.

CONTENTS

PAGE

Municipal Politics in Pompeii 3

The Story of Two Oligarchies 22

Women and Public Affairs under the Roman Republic 41

Roman Women in the Trades and Professions 77

The Theatre as a Factor in Roman Politics under the Republic 100

Petronius: A Study in Ancient Realism 115

A Roman Puritan 131

Petrarch's Letters to Cicero 145

Literature and the Common People of Rome 159

The Career of a Roman Student . . . 191

PAGE

Some Spurious Inscriptions and Their Authors 215

The Evolution of the Modern Forms of the Letters of Our Alphabet . . 234

Index 261

SOCIETY AND POLITICS IN ANCIENT ROME

MUNICIPAL POLITICS IN POMPEII

OF the three colleges of officials which most towns in Italy show, Pompeii had only the chief magistrates, who presided over the local senate and popular assembly, and the market officials. With the functions of these officers and the method of electing them we have acquired some familiarity from a study of Roman epitaphs, but most of our definite information on these points comes from the model municipal law which Julius Cæsar drew up the year before his death and from the charters of the towns of Salpensa and Malaca found near Malaga, Spain, in 1861.[1] But from none of these sources do we get much light upon the meth-

[1] The bronze tablets containing these last two documents were discovered beneath the surface of the ground carefully wrapped and protected by tiles. Their condition suggests a romance connected with their history which it would be interesting to have further light upon. They were evidently hidden to save them, and it looks as if we owed their preservation to an overruling Providence accomplishing its purpose through the dread of some tyrant. Did the people of Salpensa and Malaca hide their charters to save them, as our fathers in Connecticut did, and was Domitian, under whom they were originally granted, or some one of his tools, the Roman Governor Andrus whom the

ods which candidates for town offices used in securing a nomination and in canvassing for votes, or upon the actual state of municipal politics under the Roman Empire. For information upon these matters we must turn to the political notices found on the walls of Pompeii. Almost fifteen hundred of these have been brought to light in the portion of the city already excavated and have been published in the great collection of Latin inscriptions or in its supplements. These notices and other similar announcements, serious and frivolous, seem to have been as numerous and as offensive to some of the Pompeians as bill-boards in our modern cities are to us, for an indignant citizen has scratched on a wall in one of the streets: "I wonder, O wall, that you have not fallen in ruins from supporting the tiresome productions of so many writers." [1] It will be remembered that the Romans deposited the ashes of their dead by the side of the roads leading from the city, and the tombstones and monuments which were raised

people of these two towns sought to circumvent? It is impossible to answer these questions, but they suggest an interesting episode in the struggle for liberty.

[1] Admiror, O pariens, te non cecidisse ruinis qui tot scriptorum taedia sustineas, 1904. (All the references, unless otherwise indicated, are to Vol. IV of the *Corpus Inscriptionum Latinarum*.)

over them often furnished too tempting a location for a political poster to be resisted. A monument near Rome bears the inscription: "Bill-poster, I beg you to pass this monument by. If any candidate's name shall have been painted upon it may he suffer defeat and may he never win any office."[1]

Most of these notices are painted upon the stucco of the house walls, as is well known, in great letters from two to twelve inches tall. Those who wrote them were not members of the local senate, but private citizens of Pompeii. This fact points to the participation of the common people in the choice of their magistrates, a state of things which surprises one at first because at Rome, in the reign of Tiberius, the election of consuls was transferred from the popular assembly to the senate. Evidently the municipalities were more retentive of republican principles than the capital. This inference is in harmony with provisions of the charter of Malaca, which call for the election of local magistrates in the popular assembly. The participation of all

[1] Inscriptor rogo te ut transeas hoc monumentum . . . quoius candidati nomen in hoc monumento inscriptum fuerit repulsam ferat neque honorem ullum unquam gerat. Henzen 6977.

the people in the election had an interesting effect. It made it necessary for candidates, and for friends of candidates, to use every means possible to win the support of voters. What electoral methods were under the Republic we see clearly enough from Cicero's orations in defence of Murena and Plancius, who were charged with violating the election laws, and from the essay on "Candidacy for the Consulship." They consisted in organizing large parties to escort the candidate to and from his house, in gaining the support of clubs, organized for charitable and other purposes, in making electoral tours, in giving shows, or in using force or money when circumstances permitted it. The inscriptions from Pompeii introduce us to still another and very interesting method of canvassing for votes—the use of the election poster. This method of promoting the cause of a candidate, by putting encomiums of him on the walls where the passer-by can readily see them, is not very common with us, and so far as my observation goes, has not come into use in our city elections until recently, but is very generally employed in Europe.

The Pompeian posters deal with two stages

of the electoral campaign, viz., the nomination for office, and the canvassing for votes. In a typical specimen of the first class "M. Cerrinius Vatia is proposed for the ædileship by Nymphodotus and Caprasia."[1] Another inscription reveals the fact that Vatia has agreed to stand for office. This change in the situation is clear because a certain Verus announces his intention to vote for him, by writing on a house wall "To Vatia for the aedileship Verus Innoces gives his support,"[2] and such an announcement would hardly be made until Vatia had signified his willingness to be a candidate. The *professio*, or official registration of a prospective candidate, was made in Rome three weeks before the election took place; but the intentions of a candidate were known long in advance of the *professio*, so that this inscription does not necessarily fall within the three weeks preceding the election. The nomination to office came from a man's neighbors, sometimes in the form of individual requests that he allow his name to be used, sometimes in their united demand, which finds expression in such statements as

[1] M. Cerrinium Vatiam aed(ilem) Nymphodotus cum Caprasia rog(ant), 207.

[2] Vatiam aed(ilem) Verus Innoces facit, 1080.

"His neighbors propose Vatia for the ædileship,"[1] or "His neighbors nominate Tiberius Claudius Verus as duovir."[2]

The facit inscriptions, if we may so indicate those in which the verb used is *facit*, which probably indicate an intention to support a candidate at the polls, come from individual supporters, groups of neighbors, or from organizations. Modern posters are put up by political committees in a systematic way on any available board or wall. The practice was not the same in ancient times. The householder had his recommendation painted on the wall of his own house, just as citizens in our political campaigns display in their windows the likeness of their chosen candidate. This practice of course enables us to make out the political sympathies of the several quarters of Pompeii in a given campaign, just as the lithographed portraits in the windows in a particular section of a modern city show us who the favorite candidate of the quarter is. The recommendations were not necessarily painted by the householder. In fact the actual work was often done by a professional

[1] Vatiam aed. vicini, 443.

[2] Ti. Claudium Verum II vir vicini rogant, 367.

painter. One candidate, indeed, seems to have had his recommendations painted on the walls of his supporters' houses at his own expense, and in one inscription the four painters who did the work for him have immortalized themselves by adding their own names and by indicating that all the posters of the candidate in question are their work: "Messenio nominates M. Cerrinius Vatia as ædile—a man worthy of the commonwealth. Infantio, Florus, Fructus, and Sabinus have painted the announcement, doing the work here and everywhere."[1] In one case even the whitewasher who prepared the rectangular space on the wall as a background for the red letters of the notice has left us his name.[2]

Most of these inscriptions indicate the decision or proposed action of some person, but in a few cases they are addressed to some prominent citizen and solicit his support for the writer's candidate. So in one case we read an anonymous address to a certain Pansa: "Pansa, vote for Modestus for the ædileship!"[3]

Near the house of another citizen, Proculus,

[1] M. Cerrinium Vatiam aed. dignum rei (pub.) Messenio rog. Scripsit Infantio cum Floro et Fructo et Sabino. Hic et ubique, 230.

[2] No. 222.

[3] Modestum aed. Pans(a) fac facias, 1071.

where he would see it on going out and coming in, is painted the inscription: "Proculus, do your duty by your friend Fronto!"[1] Since proposing a candidate for office was not an official act we are not surprised to find the names of women in inscriptions of this class: "M. Casellius and L. Albucius are nominated by Statia and Petronia. May such citizens always be found in the colony!"[2] This is, by the way, one of the few recommendations in which the names of more than one candidate appear. The formal presentation of a ticket for all the offices was unknown. In fact the co-operation of two candidates was regarded with suspicion. Sometimes we can make out who the successful candidates were. In one case, for instance, an enthusiastic supporter of Proculus announces on a wall after an election that "all the Pompeians have voted for Proculus."[3] There is no indication that the imperial government had begun yet to meddle in the municipal elections, although in one instance an effort is made to use the favorable

[1] Procule Frontoni tuo officium commoda, 920.

[2] M. Casellium et L. Albucium Statia et Petronia rog. Tales cives in colonia in perpetuo, 3294.

[3] Paquium Proculum II vir i. d. d. r. p. universi Pompeiani fecerunt, 1122.

opinion of an imperial commissioner in support of M. Epidius Sabinus who is characterized as "the bulwark of the town, as Suedius Clemens the respected (federal) judge considers him, and worthy of the commonwealth on account of his merits and his uprightness in the opinion of the senate."[1] Suedius Clemens showed what would be regarded to-day as pernicious activity on the part of a federal office-holder, because in three posters his intention to vote for M. Epidius Sabinus is announced.

The most interesting recommendations, however are those which are made by organizations of one kind or another. Twenty or more of these groups figure in the posters. Most of them are made up of men engaged in the same occupation. The goldsmiths have their candidate, the dealers in fruit, the bakers, the fish-mongers, the fullers, the dyers, the barbers, the copyists, the porters, and even the priests of Isis. It seems to me hazardous to assume, as is commonly supposed, that these recommendations represent the formal action of the guilds concerned. In

[1] Defensor coloniae ex sententia Suedi Clementis sancti iudicis consensu ordinis ob merita eius et probitatem dignus rei publicae, 768. *Cf.* also 791 and 1059.

many cases, at least, they very likely indicate nothing more than the unchallenged opinion of a group of artisans or dealers. Possibly in some cases an individual has taken the responsibility of speaking for men of his calling. It would seem hardly probable, for instance, that the poster "the farmers nominate M. Casellius Marcellus as ædile" [1] points to the official support of Marcellus by the farmers. This action on the part of men belonging to the several trades naturally leads us to ask what the issues were. Negatively it may be said that in the posters we find no suggestion of the questions which ordinarily arise in a modern municipal election. No mention is made of clean streets, of paving or public buildings, of police protection, or of the water supply. No promise is made on behalf of a candidate that he will give elaborate games, supervise the markets with care, or let the public contracts honestly, although all these matters came under the control of the local officials, and were topics of very lively interest to the average citizen in the small towns, as one sees clearly from the conversations of the Cumæan freedmen at Trimalchio's dinner. What ques-

[1] M. Casellium Marcellum aed. agricolae rog., 490.

tions, then, were uppermost? Apparently those of local pride, personal popularity, and guild politics. The municipalities were divided on a territorial basis into *curiae*, or tribes, as one sees from the municipal charters, and a strong feeling of solidarity had developed in each one of these wards or districts, which led to the united support by the citizens of a ward of one of their own number for political office. To understand this situation it is only necessary to recall the survival of strong sectional feeling found in many Italian towns to-day. The fierce rivalry of the several wards in Siena, for instance, which finds expression in the annual *Palio* is but one illustration among many of the strength which the sentiment of local patriotism may take under favorable circumstances. Of course candidates who were well known and respected had an advantage over their less fortunate rivals. The esteem, for instance, in which such men as Holconius Priscus were held, whose ancestors had been honored with municipal office for half a century, or the uprightness of such a candidate as Q. Bruttius Balbus, of whom it is said in a poster "he will guard the treasury,"[1] would

[1] Hic aerarium conservabit, *Eph. Epigr.*, I, No. 163.

draw men to their support, as soon as their names were announced among those of the candidates. A reputation for integrity in his business dealings naturally improved the chances of an aspirant for office. A supporter of Julius Polybius recommended him to the favorable consideration of his fellow-citizens, because "he supplied good bread." [1]

What motives brought the dyers, fullers, and barbers to the support of a candidate must be largely a matter of surmise. It may have been some trade advantage or some promised market concession, or possibly these trade groups in some cases were supporting their patron, or at least a citizen who had served them in the past. In modern times the activity which many keepers of inns and wine-shops showed in Pompeii in furthering the interests of certain candidates would raise the suspicion that they hoped to get illicit privileges from them, but that assumption is hardly possible for Pompeii.

Among the group inscriptions two or three are found which deserve passing mention. One reads "I beg you to support A. Vettius Firmus as ædile. He deserves well of the

[1] C. Iulium Polybium aed. o. v. f. Panem bonum fert, 429.

state. I ask for your support. Ball-players, support him."[1] Other still more astonishing recommendations are found in the announcements: "All the sleepy men nominate Vatia as ædile," "the petty thieves propose Vatia for the ædileship," and "I ask your support for M. Cerrinius Vatia for the ædileship. All the late drinkers nominate him. Florus and Fructus painted this notice."[2] We are not surprised at the eagerness which Firmus's friend shows to win the support of the ball-players. They were held in high favor by the people. One of them in his epitaph celebrates his popularity, and records the fact that he had played ball frequently with the emperor.[3] As for the "sleepy-heads," the "sneak thieves," and the "heavy drinkers," the support of such people is sought to-day by some politicians, but they are studiously kept in the background for fear of frightening away serious citizens. Shall we conclude that the Pompeians were less scrupulous or fastidious on this point than we are? The city was

[1] A. Vettium Firmum aed(ilem) o(ro) v(os) f(aciatis). Dignum rei publicae. O(ro) v(os) f(aciatis). Pilicrepi facite, 1147.

[2] Vatiam aed. rogant . . . dormientes universi, 575; Vatiam aed. furunculi rog., 576; M. Cerrinium Vatiam aed. o. v. f. Seribibi universi rogant. Scr(ipsit) Florus cum Fructo, 581.

[3] *CIL.* VI, 9797.

a wicked one, and its people were surprisingly frank in recognizing the existence of human vices and weaknesses, and scholars seem to be agreed in regarding these three recommendations as striking illustrations of Pompeian depravity or of Latin frankness in such matters. In this conclusion they find confirmation in the fact that the placard of the "heavy drinkers" was put on the wall by the professional painters Florus and Fructus, who, as we have noticed above, were working in the interest of Vatia. This hypothesis, however, seems to me to put too great a strain on our credulity. Is it possible that Vatia was the candidate of the underworld, and stood for a "wide open town"? That explanation seems improbable, because some of his supporters whose names appear in other posters were men of standing in the community. Possibly these organizations are social clubs which have taken humorous names, or have good-humoredly accepted a sobriquet given them by others, but there would seem to be no parallel to such a name in any of the other hundreds of guild and club inscriptions which have come down to us. It is much more probable that all three posters are the work of a wag or of a malicious opponent of Vatia who wished to intimate that all the bad elements in the city were rallying to his support. The announcement at the end of the third notice that Vatia's employees, "Florus and Fructus, painted it" would only show a keener sense of humor on the part of the supposed wag, or would be a more convincing proof of the authenticity of the placard in the eyes of the passer-by, if it emanates from one of Vatia's enemies. This explanation is supported by the fact that these three recommendations are all found in the same street and, therefore, may well be the work of the same person. A friend suggests that the same humorous or malicious hand was at work in painting the inscription quoted above, "To Vatia for the ædileship Verus Innoces gives his support," and that this supporter of Vatia existed only in the imagination of the composer of the notice. If we accept this conjecture we may be sure that the quick-witted Pompeian would see the point in the statement that Verus Innoces, or "the truly guileless man," was supporting Vatia in his candidacy for the office of police commissioner, especially when he read on neighboring walls the endorsements which

Vatia had received from the three groups mentioned above.

The tendency of the Roman to drop into stereotyped formulæ, especially in the inscriptions, is abundantly illustrated in the political notices. One would think from reading them that the Latin language had no phrases of approbation save *dignus rei publicae*, *vir bonus*, and *iuvenis probus*. These three locutions, with scarcely a variant, are reiterated again and again. Recommendations with these conventional formulæ scarcely suggest a spontaneous outburst of enthusiasm on the part of the writer, but the formulæ had the merit, which would recommend them to the practical Roman, of being so well known that they could be abbreviated, to the great saving of time and space. Among these recurring phrases of high esteem now and then a sentiment is expressed which suggests other than patriotic motives on the part of some of the voters. Thus a certain Rufinus is asked to "vote for Popidius Secundus and Secundus will vote for him," and in other inscriptions the friends of candidates are warned to be on their guard. The warning is evidently directed against bribery or other illegal means of securing votes.

After all, the first purpose of a political system is to secure good government. In this the Pompeians seem to have been successful. The condition of the streets, of the public buildings, and of the water works all go to show it. This leads us to another consideration which is not without interest. The charter which Domitian gave to Malaca provided that, if the number of candidates who had registered their names with the magistrate chosen to hold the elections was not large enough to fill the required offices, he should of his own motion make the necessary additions to the list. Thereupon the men whose names had been added could make further nominations, and the second set of nominees could propose other candidates still. This article in Domitian's charter points very clearly to a growing disinclination on the part of citizens to accept office, a disinclination which became so great that by the close of the second century municipal officials were picked out by the outgoing magistrates, and the choice thus made was formally ratified, not by the popular assembly, which henceforth has no part in the elections, but by the local senate. The reasons for this disinclination to hold office, and for the loss of popular interest in the elections, are various. First of all, a magistrate was called upon to contribute generously to the games in his year of office, as one can see from the charter of the town of Urso in Spain. Furthermore, the extravagant municipal improvements which many towns introduced in the second century of our era left their finances in a hopeless condition, and the task of a city official in managing them must have been difficult and disagreeable. Finally, the central government, through its representatives, assumed so many functions which the local government had exercised before that the dignity of a municipal office and the interest of the people in the choice of their magistrates naturally disappeared at the same time. Pompeii shows no sign of this downward movement. The large number of political posters testifies at the same time to lively popular interest in the elections and to a spirited contest between candidates for office. These very posters lent a dignity to the municipal magistracies. They run from the time of Augustus down to 79 A. D., the year of the eruption, and were permanent memorials of the esteem in which certain men had been held by their fellow-citizens. Like the lists of the consuls on the walls of the Regia at Rome they contained a record, which was always before the eyes of the people of Pompeii, of those who had been honored with office and of those whom a large number of citizens would have liked to see so honored.

THE STORY OF TWO OLIGARCHIES

WHAT sudden and radical changes time brings upon us! Only a few years ago a very clever book appeared establishing the fact that the Speaker of the lower house of Congress controlled the political policy of the nation. One could not dispute the conclusion. In the palmy days of Randall and Carlisle the House ruled at Washington and the Speaker ruled the House. The country waited to hear his choice of Chairman for the Committee of Ways and Means and for the Committee on Appropriations to know whether he and his advisers had decided to give the nation free trade or protection, to prescribe an economical or a liberal policy for the coming two years. His faithful supporters on the floor were rewarded with committee assignments which gave them prestige in the House and before the people. His open enemies, when such could be found, or the men whose hostility could be neglected, were shelved in the Committee on Weights and Measures.

How the House has fallen from its high estate and the Speaker with it! Who cares in these days whether it favors or opposes a judicial review of the decisions of the Inter-State Commerce Commission, whether it proposes the placing of hides on the free list or the imposition of a duty on them? The settlement of such matters now rests with its lord and master at the other end of the Capitol. The senators wink at one another, as did the Roman augurs, when even such a skilful leader and clever tactician as Speaker Cannon announces his intention to have the House treated as a co-ordinate legislative body. If the Senate is in a generous mood, by making some trifling concessions in the matter of form to the conferees from the House, it may allow the Speaker to "save his face," as the Washington correspondents put it. This gracious course it took in the statehood dispute in 1908 and won the gratitude of the House by its condescension, but concessions on points of serious moment a sovereign can hardly be expected to make. To the House the situation is a *fait accompli.* The measures which it sends up to the Senate are like petitions to a ruler, to be received and enacted into laws with radical changes, if the Senate finds something of merit in them, or rejected altogether, or left unconsidered in committee. That the House accepts the situation seems to be clear from the loose form in which it leaves important propositions like the rate bill. Why spend time in perfecting a measure when the real business of legislation is carried on elsewhere? Why trouble one's self with consistency, completeness, or constitutionality, when another body will settle all these questions as seems best to it? And yet the House finds useful work to do under the new interpretation of the Constitution. The projects which are laid before it and the discussions which take place in it are published throughout the country, and the Senate has an opportunity to learn the trend and the strength of public sentiment before it takes up a matter for action. It is rarely obliged, therefore, to change its attitude toward a question on account of an unexpectedly strong popular feeling against its course. Furthermore, since the House is carried along more easily than the Senate by the current of public opinion, and since it can take action quickly, inasmuch as it would be useless labor for it to take time to perfect its measures, the Senate rarely finds it necessary to initiate important legislation, but can wait until public opinion has been tested through the medium of the House. The late Speaker Reed is said to have thanked God that "the House was not a deliberative body." Were he living now he might express thankfulness or regret that it is not a legislative body.

This elimination of the House from the control of the government has narrowed down the struggle for supremacy to the Senate and the President, just as the death of Crassus in the waning years of the Roman Republic brought the other two members of the First Roman Triumvirate face to face, precipitated a conflict between them, and made the triumph of Cæsar or Pompey inevitable. This second stage in the Senate's struggle for supremacy is intensified by a variety of circumstances. That the struggle of the Senate for the mastery had reached this second stage was brought into bold relief during the closing months of President Roosevelt's administration. He held positive views on public questions and insisted upon them vigorously. Few political or social abuses escaped his eye, and a fair catalogue of the evils of the day, with remedies for them, might be drawn up from his messages and personal letters. This passion for reform was caviare to so conservative a body as the Senate. To make the matter worse the great majority which he received at the ballot-box made him in a peculiar sense the tribune of the people, and in his contest with the Senate he believed that public opinion supported him. Then, too, as if in anticipation of the future, on the night of his election he had announced that he would not accept a renomination, and thus made it known that the fear of arousing enmities which would prejudice his political future would not influence his action. It has been remarked also that no one of his predecessors took so active a part in the actual work of legislation as he did. Whether this was true or not, probably no president intervened in legislative matters in so public a way. In fact, the element of publicity was one of the noteworthy features of the struggle, and drew tight the lines of battle between the parties to the contest. He made a legislative project his own cause, and his personal leadership in the fight for a rate bill, a pure-food law, or a Santo

Domingo bill, was recognized by both its friends and its enemies. It happened, too, that most of the issues which arose between the President and the Senate were issues upon which a deep interest was felt throughout the country.

The present occupant of the presidential chair has a very different temperament from his predecessor, consequently he is not likely to arouse the personal antagonism of the members of the Senate by an impassioned advocacy of his views, by impatient treatment of his opponents, by attempting to control too specifically the form which legislation shall take, or by asserting in too positive a way the rights of the executive branch of the government. This difference in methods of procedure will probably lessen the acuteness of the struggle, and obscure to some extent in the minds of the people the fact that a contest exists. But President Taft is a man of positive convictions, and his views upon matters of public interest, like the tariff, the imposition of an income tax, Philippine policy, or the regulation of interstate commerce may well be at variance with those of the Senate. In fact, although the intensity of the conflict may vary from one presidential term to another, a conflict is inevitable when two branches of the government are brought face to face as rivals for supremacy. What will be the outcome of the struggle? Shall we pass over to an oligarchical form of government, or to a democratic empire?

One is tempted to turn back in history to another great struggle between an ambitious oligarchy and a chief magistrate, to the struggle between the Roman senate and consul, to see if it will throw any light on our own political future. The comparison is tempting because the Roman oligarchy, like our own, had to face a legislative and an executive rival, and history gives us in some detail the story of its contest with both of its competitors. The similar character of the two cases is the more striking because in its essence the Roman governmental system was not unlike our own, and because the relation of the three contending parties was nearly the same as it is with us. In their senate and popular assembly the Romans had practically a bicameral system. Within certain limits bills, after approval by the senate, were laid before the assembly for adoption or rejection. The two branches of the legislature were independent of each other. One was popular in its character; the other was a body of picked men, farther removed from public opinion. The consul, like our president, was an elective officer, and not a minister whose term of office could be cut short by the one or the other legislative body. It would be interesting to compare the circumstances which gave the Roman senate its ascendency over its legislative rival with the corresponding situation in this country, but the triumph of our own Senate over the House, whether permanent or temporary, is complete. Our interest lies in the battle which is on, not in the contest which is settled, so that we shall confine ourselves to a comparison in its broad outlines of the struggle between the Roman senate and consul and the one which we have lately seen and are likely to see in the future, between our own Senate and the President.

We have already observed in a general way that the constitutional relations between the oligarchy and the chief magistrate in the two cases are similar. This fact will be still more apparent if we compare the membership and functions of the ancient and the modern body.

Roman senators did not inherit their positions, nor were they appointed to them, but they received them by election. This common characteristic differentiates the Roman senate and our own Senate from most upper houses in ancient and modern times, but the choice of senators in Rome was not made directly by the people any more than it is with us. The great majority of our senators are experienced politicians, and have held their seats for many years. This was true of Roman senators also. Many of our senators are rich men; so were the Roman senators, and one of the two bodies could be called a rich man's club as properly as the other.

A still more characteristic point of resemblance lies in the existence of a strong *esprit de corps* in both bodies. Senatorial courtesy was as marked in Rome as it is in Washington, and made senators stand as a unit against the administration when the claims of their order or their individual rights or privileges were involved. Perhaps this sentiment was even stronger in the Roman body than it is in our Upper House, for its members constituted a class recognized by law, a class with power to transmit some of its privileges to its descendants. In this connection two or three peculiarities in Roman parliamentary procedure are interesting. In its palmy days the senate kept no minutes, did not require a quorum, and did not have motions set down in writing. This is a strange state of affairs among a people so methodical as the Romans and so gifted with political genius as they were. It does not indicate a high state of political honor among them, for corruption and chicanery were rife in politics, but it is a striking testimony to the *esprit de corps* of the senate. Evidently these lax methods of doing business had come down from early times, and it had never been found necessary to revise them. A long experience with them had shown that no matter what party advantages or personal privileges were at stake a member would observe the principles of senatorial courtesy and the traditions of the senate. When he elaborated his motion and set it down in written form after the adjournment of the senate he could be trusted not to change the essential character which he had given to it in his oral statement. This feeling of solidarity was strengthened in the Roman senate and is supported in our Upper House by a long and honorable tradition, and by noteworthy achievements for the state. The office of chief executive has no such traditional meaning. It was the individual consul Cicero who suppressed the Catilinarian conspiracy, or the individual President Lincoln who issued the proclamation of emancipation; but it is the Roman senate or the United States Senate which, by its power to ratify treaties and confirm appointments, controlled foreign relations before the birth of a Cicero or a Lincoln, and will control them after the brief term of a particular chief executive is ended. The cumulative effect of such a long line of achievements cannot be overestimated. Presidents may come and presidents may go, but the Senate goes on forever.

We have taken warning from Roman history in one respect. In our dread of Cæsarism, popular prejudice has limited the president's tenure of office to eight years, but we have not noticed the Roman senator's long term of office, and studied its effect on democratic government in Rome. Cicero and Catulus held their positions as senators for a quarter of a century, and their length of service was by no means exceptional. They became thoroughly familiar with the traditions of the senate, and were always watching to maintain and extend its dignity and influence. Their familiarity with precedents and with the transaction of business, even more than their ability, gave them a recognized leadership in the body to which they belonged. They had succeeded another group of experienced leaders, and would be followed by men like unto themselves. They gave continuity to the policy of the Roman senate, just as the Hales, Aldriches, and Culloms preserve inviolate the traditions of our Senate. There is no such element of continuity in the presidency any more than there was in the consulship. A chief executive with a limited term of office scarcely learns where his strength and weakness lie before he must give way to a successor. His attention is centred rather upon the carrying out of the promises which he has made to the electors, upon the preservation of party unity, or the furtherance of his chances for renomination, than upon the maintenance and extension of the dignity of the presidential office. The prestige of the position suffers, as did that of the consulship, in consequence of this difference of purpose which characterizes the two contending parties.

We have noticed briefly the similarity between the Roman senate and our own in the matter of membership and character. Let us look at the characteristic functions of the two bodies. One source of power which the Senate of the United States uses most effectively in coercing the President is its right to confirm appointments. Thanks to this privilege almost all our federal officials are chosen by senators, not by the President, and the Senate's political influence and its control of the administration is thereby tremendously strengthened. The Roman senate used the same weapon against the consul with like effect. Governorships abroad and other important appointive offices were given to men who were faithful to the senate, and those who opposed it suffered for their temerity. A recalcitrant consul of Cicero's day, for instance, lost the great prize of the governorship of Asia for his rashness in making some political speeches against a measure which the senate favored. Cæsar, too, who opposed the senate during his consulship, would have had a forest and a marsh for his province at the end of his term of office, if the senate had had its way. So clearly did Gaius Gracchus, the great opponent of the senate, understand this fact, that he made a determined onslaught upon the senate's power to use the offices in rewarding its friends and maintaining its prestige.

At the meeting on January 1, when the legislative year opened, the presiding consul made a statement on the condition of the commonwealth, and laid before the senate the matters which he thought deserved its consideration, very much as our President does in his messages. The Roman senate well understood that nothing discredits an administration so completely as to thwart its policy by rejecting or shelving its proposals, or by adopting them in such a form that their author scarcely knows whether to accept the substitutes or not. In refusing at a late session to pass bills establishing a protectorate over Santo Domingo, regulating insurance, and in its treatment of President Roosevelt's plan for the regulation of railway rates, the Senate was following a course which its prototype followed on many occasions. It makes little difference whether the motives which actuate a legislative body in such action are patriotic or selfish, the chief executive is chagrined, his failure is apparent to the country, and the importance of the law-making body is exalted at his expense.

We had occasion to say something above, by way of illustration, of the control of foreign affairs by the Roman senate and our own. It is an interesting fact that Roman tradition and that the Constitution of this country gave the popular branch of the legislature no share in the conduct of foreign affairs. So long as we followed our policy of isolation the Senate's right to accept or reject a treaty was of comparatively small importance; but now that we have become a world power, have acquired colonies in remote parts, have assumed a quasi-protectorate over our neighbors to the south, and have even ventured into the arena of European politics, as we did in taking part in the Algeciras Conference, this function of the Senate acquires an added importance, and the Senate is not unmindful of the new chance to increase its power which the change in national policy has thrown in its way. Its treatment of arbitration and reciprocity treaties has shown the President that it and not he controls our permanent relations with foreign countries. The President's power to negotiate treaties has gone the way of his power to appoint to office. It was so in Rome. The consul represented the nation in its dealings with foreign powers, but the senate easily reduced him to the position of an intermediary between itself and the representatives of the state concerned, and as Roman interests abroad increased, the influence of the senate was correspondingly augmented, and at the expense of the chief executive.

The Senate of the United States is almost alone among great legislative bodies in not adopting clôture. The history of the last few years bears eloquent witness to the advantage under the bicameral system enjoyed by the body which allows unlimited debate over the co-ordinate assembly which limits discussion. Perhaps the downfall of the House may be traced more directly to its introduction of clôture than to any other one cause. A bare majority may push a bill through the House, but it may fail utterly in the Senate, as did the Force Bill, and the Ship Subsidy Bill, or it may be exasperatingly delayed or radically amended unless it satisfies all the members in the Upper House. Consequently a bill, to become a law, must meet the wishes of the Senate rather than of the House. This parliamentary weapon can be used with equal effect against a chief magistrate, as the history of the Senate during the last few years abundantly shows. Strangely enough the Roman senate allowed its members the same privilege. On a certain occasion, the irrepressible Cato was filibustering against an agrarian measure which the presiding consul, Cæsar, was very anxious to pass. Cæsar ordered the sergeant-at-arms to remove him. Cato was removed, but the entire senate followed him from the house, and no magistrate ever again attempted to limit debate.

Making use of the tactical advantages which we have outlined above — and our Senate has the same elements of strength — the Roman senate, as we know, reduced the chief magistrate to the position of its minister, and made itself undisputed master of the state. Tiberius Gracchus, to whom President Roosevelt has lately been compared, first ventured to question its supremacy, and the uprising against the senatorial oligarchy which he organized attained its success in the next century in the democratic empire of Julius Cæsar. Among the immediate causes which contributed to the downfall of the Roman senate, two stand out with special prominence, its class prejudice and its inefficiency. It represented the wealth and the aristocracy of the times. It was strangely deaf to public sentiment. It opposed popular leaders like the Gracchi and Cæsar without justice or tact, and failed to notice that the tide was setting toward democracy. It was chauvinistic in its foreign policy, as our own Senate has shown itself at times — in its treatment of arbitration treaties, for instance — and this attitude was not adapted to further the interests of the whole empire. Its second point of weakness, its inefficiency, was apparent not so much in its failure to manage the government well, as in its failure to manage itself. One of its chief sources of strength in its struggle with its rivals became in the end a fatal source of weakness. In the last few years of the Republic a dozen instances are recorded in which a single member by "talking against time" prevented his colleagues from taking the action which they desired. It was, in fact, the obstructive tactics of Cato on the occasion mentioned above which drove Cæsar to put an end to the intolerable situation by ignoring the senate and by carrying his measures in the popular assembly in spite of senatorial opposition. This step broke the primacy of the senate, and that body never regained its prestige. For the sake of completeness we have followed the story of the Roman senate to the end. It would be rash to predict a like outcome at some future day in the struggle between the Senate and the President, but the fable teaches us that eternal vigilance is the price of liberty.

WOMEN AND PUBLIC AFFAIRS UNDER THE ROMAN REPUBLIC

SOME day the story of the "emancipation" of the Roman woman will be told. It will set forth the steps by which she gradually freed herself from the mastery of the *paterfamilias*, gained control of her dower, the privilege of holding property in her own name, and, except for the absence of political rights, a more favored position before the law than her husband held. I have no intention of attempting to tell that story here. My purpose is merely to bring together a few facts from the history of the late Republic, that may throw some light upon the rôle which women played in the political life of the Roman people during that period.

Tombstones record the virtues of many Roman matrons, and it is easy to see from them what the Roman's ideal of womanhood was and what he thought properly fell within and outside the range of a woman's activities. The prevailing sentiment is illustrated by the well-known epitaph on the tomb of Claudia outside the walls of Rome: "Stranger, what I have to say is quickly told; stop, and read it to the end. Here is the unbeautiful tomb of a beautiful woman. Claudia was the name her parents gave her. Her husband she loved with her whole heart. Two sons she bore; of them the one she leaves on earth, the other she buried beneath the sod. Charming in discourse, gentle in mien, she kept the house, she made the wool. I have finished. Go thy way." Claudia was the devoted wife and mother, who gave an air of grace and charm to the home life, and skilfully directed the affairs of the household. She was the ideal matron of the good old days, whose influence on public life came from the example which she set to others in performing faithfully and well the duties which fell to her lot, from the respect which her husband had for her judgment, and from the training which she gave her sons.

But time brought changes with it. Roman women never won nor claimed an equal share with men in public affairs, but they found means, as civilization advanced, to make their influence felt more and more directly and effectively in the management of them. However, even in the stormy days of early Rome, when the mailed hand ruled, tradition is fond of recording the large part which women played in the affairs of state. It recounts to us in the pages of Livy the pathetic story of Horatia and her Alban lover, and the heroic death of Lucretia, with its tragic results for the line of Tarquin. It gives us the story of Tarquinia, the Roman prototype of the notorious Catherine of Russia, whose boldly conceived plans and whose determination, unweakened by a single touch of justice or of mercy, carried her husband to the throne. It sketches for us the masterful and resourceful Tanaquil, who saved the realm for her foster-son, Servius Tullius, and directed him perhaps in those great reforms which have made his name famous in the early history of the city on the Palatine.

It is a pleasant thing to turn from the deeds of violence which the names of Horatia, Tarquinia, and Lucretia suggest, and to recall the fact that the first woman mentioned in the legendary history of the city of Rome was an apostle of peace, and a successful one, too. When a Sabine people, enraged at the treacherous seizure of their women at a festival, had rashly entered Roman territory, had been overwhelmed by the army of Romulus, and were face to face with the cruel treatment which the primitive practices of war prescribed for the conquered, Hersilia, the wife of Romulus, in the name of the Sabine wives of the Romans, met her victorious husband as he entered the city on his triumphant return from the campaign, and prevailed upon him to pardon her kinsmen and even to make them Roman citizens. It is a pleasant thing to recall the fact that Numa, the prototype of the righteous, peace-loving king, drew his inspiration from Egeria, and that her counsel directed him in the policy which made Rome for many years, as the myth of Numa tells us, a mighty influence for peace and harmony throughout central Italy. Perhaps in real life there was never an Hersilia who prevailed upon her husband to make peace. The story that Tanaquil quieted the people after the death of Tarquin by her clever speech from the upper story of the palace may be a pure myth; but the Roman of a later day, when the legends of the early period grew up, evidently thought these situations not improbable, or he would not have made them a part of the history of Rome.

When women do first appear on the political stage in historical times it must be confessed that the setting is not quite so romantic nor is the cause for which they stand so serious as is the case with these women of prehistoric days, yet the movement which they lead is more characteristically feminine. The date is 195 B.C., and the question at issue a sumptuary law. Just after the disastrous battle of Cannæ, when Rome needed to use all her resources against Hannibal, and when a display of wealth by the rich might have stimulated a class feeling which would have been disastrous in the national emergency, the Oppian law was passed forbidding any woman to have more than half an ounce of gold, to wear a parti-colored garment, or to ride in a chariot within the city or within a mile of it, except for religious purposes. But in 195 the stress of war was over; prosperity had returned; women wished to enjoy their privileges once more, and succeeded in persuading two of the tribunes to propose the repeal of the law. But they did not content themselves with this preliminary move. The bold methods which they used in carrying their plans to a successful issue shocked the sedate historian Livy, who tells us that the matrons could be kept at home neither by persuasion, nor by a sense of modesty, nor by the authority of their husbands. They blocked up all the streets of the city and the approaches to the Forum, importuning men as they came down to the Forum to vote for the restoration of their rights. The leader of the party opposed to them was Cato, who held display in dress and the new woman in like abhorrence. These are the two topics upon which he descants in his indignant speech against the repeal of the law. He cynically asks the women: "Are your ways more winning in public than in private, and with other women's husbands than your own? And yet not even at home ought you to concern yourselves with the laws which are passed or repealed here. Our fathers have not wished women to manage even their private affairs without the direction of a guardian; they have wanted them to be under the control of their parents, their brothers, and their husbands. We, by our present action, if the gods permit it, are letting them go into politics even; we are letting them appear in the Forum, and take a hand at public meetings and in the voting booths." Cato closes his appeal to the men with this gloomy picture of the future: "Pray, what will they not assail, if they carry this point? Call to mind all the principles governing them by which your ancestors have held the presumption of women in check, and made them subject to their husbands. Though they have been restrained by all these, still you can scarcely keep them in bounds. Tell me, if you let them seize privileges and wrest them from you one by one, and finally become your equals, do you think that you can stand them? As soon as they have begun to be your equals they will be your superiors." Lucius Valerius, the champion of the women, replied to this fiery oration of Cato by recounting the sacrifices which women had made for the state in the past, and by asserting that they were not now taking a hand in public affairs for the first time, and that they should have a share in the good times which had returned to the city. "Magistracies, priesthoods, triumphs, insignia of office, the prizes and spoils of war may not come to them," he said. "Elegance in adornment and dress — these are their insignia; in these they delight and glory."

Two of the tribunes had announced their intention to veto the repeal bill, and in their final tactics the Roman women seem to have anticipated political methods which are not unknown to-day. They beset the doors of these officials in a solid phalanx, and did not give over their demonstration until the tribunes promised not to oppose them. The repeal bill was passed by unanimous vote in the assembly, and Cassius Dio, the historian, tells us that "the women put on some ornaments right there in the assembly and went out dancing."

From this time on to the middle of the next century a dozen or more attempts were made to limit by statute expenditure on dress, at dinners, and at funerals, but they were all ineffective. We may suspect that the silent or organized opposition of the women brought many of these measures to naught, but history throws no light on the point.

They did protest, however, a century or more later when, as Valerius Maximus tells us, no man dared take up their cause. The members of the Second Triumvirate were hard pressed for money in the year 43 B. C., in equipping an army for the impending struggle with Brutus and Cassius, and published an edict requiring fourteen hundred of the richest women to make a valuation of their property, and to contribute such portion of it as should be required. The women affected by this proclamation at first appealed to the sister of Octavianus and to the mother and the wife of Antony to enlist their support against the execution of this arbitrary measure; but meeting with only partial success, as Appian in his History of the Civil Wars tells us, they came down to the Forum, forced their way to the tribunal of the triumvirs, whose acts no man dared question, and protested vigorously through their spokesman Hortensia, the daughter of the great orator Hortensius: "Let war with the Gauls or the Parthians come," she said, "and we shall not be inferior to our mothers in zeal for the common safety; but for civil wars may we never contribute, nor even assist you against one another." It was Hortensia who enunciated on this occasion, for the first time in history, so far as I know, the principle of "no taxation without representation." "Why should we pay taxes," she cried, "when we have no part in the honors, the commands, the state-craft, for which you contend against one another with such harmful results?" Appian informs us that "when Hortensia had thus spoken the triumvirs were angry that women should dare to hold a public meeting when men were silent, . . . and they ordered the lictors to drive them away from the tribunal, which they proceeded to do until cries were raised by the multitude outside, when the lictors desisted, and the triumvirs said they would postpone till the next day the consideration of the matter."

We hear nothing more of the concerted action of large bodies of women until we come to the *conventus matronarum,* or "the little senate," as the biographer of the Emperor Heliogabalus calls it. This body held its meetings on the Quirinal, and by its decrees settled questions of dress, precedence, and the use of carriages. The ancient historians are inclined to scoff at the deliberations of this assembly, but some modern courts might not be sorry to have the troublesome questions of court dress and official etiquette decided peacefully by a majority vote of court ladies. A feminine critic might even say with some justice that the deliberations and acts of "the little senate" at this period were as important as those of the senate made up of men. Before leaving this branch of our subject it may be interesting to recall the fact that, among the political posters found on the walls of Pompeii recommending certain candidates to the attention of voters, one is signed by two women; but women do not seem to have taken a very active part in the support of political candidates.

If we knew the history of the escape of woman from her position of tutelage in the family, we should probably learn a great deal about her influence on public affairs. Unfortunately we know only the concrete results, not the influences which brought them about. The betterment in her condition was a natural result of the advance of civilization, and possibly all the advantages which she had gained by the middle of the first century B. C. would have come to her even if she had remained passive and contented with her position. In point of fact much of the improvement in her lot resulted from a change in public sentiment which found no expression in law. And yet there were certain statutes which materially improved her position, and the fact that we know nothing of organized support of these measures by women would seem to be merely an accident of history. The vigorous and successful attack which we have seen them making on a sumptuary law in the second century, and their protest against taxation in the first century before our era, make it reasonably certain that they would actively support those projects of law which would give them a greater measure of liberty and happiness in their everyday life. The great improvement which woman's position in the family underwent will be clear if we call to mind her status in the early period. Her consent to a marriage was not necessary; the matter was arranged by the fathers of the bride and bridegroom. On marrying she passed under the complete control of her husband, who could, with the approval of the family council, inflict corporal punishment on her, or even put her to death. Her property passed into her husband's hands and her earnings became his; he could dispose of his estate by will as he pleased, and, under the best conditions, as an heir to her husband's property she stood on the basis of a daughter, and the inheritance which came to her was managed by a guardian appointed under the will. In course of time the conception of marriage upon which these practices rested underwent a complete change. The theory grew up that marriage was a contract which, like other contracts, required the free consent of the two people concerned, and could be dissolved if they wished it. As in other partnerships, the two contracting parties stood on an equal footing; the wife controlled her property and willed it as she pleased. Even an unmarried woman, by a fictitious marriage which was at once dissolved, could secure a guardian of her own choice, and through him manage her fortune as she pleased. It is significant that the most important of these changes, so far as they were brought about by legislation, came after the close of the Second Punic War, and, therefore, followed closely on the repeal of the Oppian law.

Although history has not left us an account of the circumstances under which these laws were passed, so that we hear little more than has been given above of the united political action of women, we *do* hear much of the great influence exerted by individual women under the late Republic. To begin with the earliest authentic instance of the sort, a woman may well be given credit for initiating the great revolution in society and government which, beginning toward the close of the second century before our era, worked itself out into the democratic empire of Julius Cæsar and the dyarchy of Augustus, for Plutarch is probably right when he intimates that Tiberius Gracchus, the forerunner of the revolution, drew his inspiration and the direct impulse to his land reforms from the teachings and admonitions of his mother Cornelia, and from what we know of her character it would seem highly probable that she trained her other son Gaius to take up the work of his brother at the point where Tiberius left it when he fell a victim to his political enemies. She spent her declining years in her villa near Misenum. Here she was visited by many of the distinguished men of the time and kept the memory of her sons alive by recounting their deeds and their hopes. Through her the cause for which Tiberius and Gaius died lived after their death, and we may well believe that some of the men who carried on their reforms went out from this little circle about Cornelia.

In the next century a woman of a far different type made her influence felt in a similar way through the circle of brilliant men whom she attracted to her. The salon of Clodia on the Palatine and in her villa on the seashore at Baiæ drew together the foremost politicians, poets, and orators of the time—men of the older generation, like Cicero and Metellus, young men like her brother Clodius, the brilliant and erratic tribune, or Cælius, whom Cicero calls "the best-informed politician in Rome." "The burning eyes" of Clodia, which Cicero celebrates in his fierce attack upon her, her brilliant wit, her versatile character, her skill as a dancer, her abandon and bohemianism, her Claudian pride and contempt for popular opinion are all marks of that fiery southern temperament which could find no middle course between love and hate, which would hesitate for no scruple and be thwarted by no obstacle from gratifying her desires or satisfying her thirst for revenge, which would be as fickle as it would be relentless toward fickleness in others. It is her glory and her misfortune that her character and exploits have been painted by the most gifted poet, the greatest orator, and one of the most brilliant wits of her time. She tired of Catullus, and he poured upon her all the vials of his wrath and scorn. She failed to ensnare

Cicero, and she avenged herself upon him by driving him into exile and taking his property from him. She was jilted and laughed at by the once-devoted Cælius, and consequently brought a charge of attempted murder against him and almost compassed his ruin. Whether she deserves the abuse which Catullus heaps upon her in his later poems, whether she merits the epitaph of the "three-cent Clytemnestra" which Cælius puts upon her, or is "the Palatine Medea" whom Cicero paints her in his defence of Cælius, we may never know. At all events she was one of the most striking figures of the period and exerted a tremendous influence upon the public life of her time, upon the fortunes of individual politicians, and upon the fate of the Republic, and this is the side of her life in which we are interested here. It will be remembered that it was the primary object of the First Triumvirate to break the prestige of the senate. This could be accomplished in no better way than by robbing it of one of its greatest leaders and by humiliating him personally. The case against him must be one which would appeal to the masses, and the hand of the triumvirs must not be disclosed in the attack.

All these conditions pointed to Cicero. He was the great orator of the senate and a recognized leader in it. He had exposed himself to popular wrath by executing the Catilinarian conspirators without granting them an appeal to the popular assembly. In Clodius circumstances put in the hands of the triumvirs the tool to be used. To accomplish his object, Clodius had himself elected to the tribunate; he brought against Cicero the charge of putting citizens to death without due process of law, and secured his banishment and the confiscation of his property. Perhaps Clodius was a radical by nature, and perhaps his political sympathies or his hope of advancement by the triumvirs induced him to make this attack upon Cicero; but the success of it called for fixity of purpose, for years of preparation, and the surmounting of innumerable obstacles, and Clodius was erratic and unstable. Who or what held him up to his purpose and drove him on through every hinderance to the accomplishment of it? Is it not probable that Clodia's savage hate for Cicero, who had repelled her advances, as Plutarch tells us, helped to keep her brother true to his purpose? Her influence over him was boundless, and, knowing her temperament, we can be sure that she would not stop until she had satisfied her desire for vengeance. This theory of the situation is strengthened by what Cicero writes to his friend Atticus in the year before his banishment of the calls to battle of "the ox-eyed one," and by the anxiety which he feels during his exile to know what she is saying and doing. It is confirmed by the vindictiveness with which she pursues Cicero's wife and daughter during his absence from Rome. Clodia had a share, then, in delivering the first fatal blow to the senate. Senatorial government would not have survived indefinitely and the revolution would have come about in time had it not been for her fierce hatred of Cicero which made itself felt through her pliant brother, but her political leadership was one of the instruments in the hands of fate which put an end to the old régime. One woman, therefore, Cornelia, set the revolution in motion; another, Clodia, brought the movement to a climax.

The period of the triumvirs saw women play a new rôle in politics. Leaders strengthened their political relations with one another by intermarriage, very much as the ruling houses of Europe do to-day, and such marriages had a profound influence on the course of events at several critical moments. The theory mentioned above, that marriage was a contract which the two parties entering into it could terminate at will, lent itself readily to the new political methods which have just been mentioned. A politician upon some plausible pretext could put away his wife, and could enter into a new marriage relation more consonant with his new political plans. Julius Cæsar seems to have been the first statesman to adopt this political policy systematically by marrying as his first wife the daughter of the democratic leader, Cinna, and upon her death by taking in marriage Pompeia, the granddaughter of Cinna's great opponent, the dictator Sulla. By this means he came into close relations with the leaders of both the great political parties. The other most noteworthy cases of the sort are those of Julia, Octavia, and Scribonia, and they deserve a moment's notice. The political compact into which Cæsar and Pompey entered at Luca in 60 B. C., known as the First Triumvirate, was cemented in the following year by the marriage of Pompey to Cæsar's daughter Julia.

Though more than twenty years younger than Pompey, her devotion to him, her beauty, and her personal charm, won her Pompey's affection and respect, and her tact preserved friendly relations between her father and her husband up to her untimely death in 54 B. C. It is a significant proof of her political influence over the triumvirs that the renewal of their agreement took place the year before her death, and that the breach between the two members of the combination who survived after the death of Crassus began within a year and a half after her decease. Pompey wished to bury her remains on his Alban estate, but the Roman people, in grateful remembrance of the service which she had rendered to the state and to the cause of peace, insisted upon giving her a public funeral and upon burying her in the Campus Martius.

So helpful had Julia been in maintaining a cordial feeling between the two leaders that on her death Cæsar offered his grand-niece Octavia in marriage to Pompey, but Pompey declined the proposal. Fate had reserved her for another political alliance and imposed upon her the rôle of an advocate of peace in still more trying circumstances. When Cæsar and Pompey passed off the stage, their places as masters of the state were taken by Octavianus and Antony, who watched each other with suspicious eyes, as Cæsar and Pompey had done. By 40 B. C. the bond which held them together was strained almost to the snapping point, but, fortunately, by the treaty of that year they were brought together again, and the clouds of civil war which had hung over the country were for the time dispelled. But the soldiers of the two armies had come to see the efficacy of political marriages, and insisted upon the marriage of Antony to Octavia, who was the sister of Octavianus. Antony, with the remembrance of Cleopatra still in his mind, hesitated, but the soldiery forced his acceptance of the proposal. The part which Octavia played from this time on in averting war is so well known that it needs no detailed recital here. When the powers of the Triumvirate expired by limitation at the close of the year 38 B. C., when Octavianus was suspicious and discourteous in his treatment of Antony, when Antony had given up all attempts to reach an understanding with him, it was Octavia who crossed over to Italy and prevailed upon her brother to renew the alliance. In the meantime Antony's relations with Cleopatra were well known in Italy and excited great indignation against him and sympathy for Octavia. Octavianus planned to augment these sentiments to his own advantage by ordering his sister to leave Antony's house where she was staying in Rome. This she firmly refused to do. Devoted as she was to Antony, stronger than her devotion to him was her desire to avert a war between her husband and her brother and to keep the East and the West in harmony. Cleopatra's object, if Ferrero's acute analysis of her policy is correct, was also political. "She hoped by marrying Antony to save Egypt from the common fate of the other Mediterranean peoples, the fate of servitude to Rome." She had tried to attain her end through Cæsar, but failing in her plan with him, sought to carry it out through Antony. It was a desperate political game played by two women for the favor of one man. Both were beautiful, brilliant, and accomplished women of the world. Both had shown themselves to be skilful women of affairs: Cleopatra, in the management of Egyptian interests and in the far-sightedness of her policy; Octavia, in securing troops and supplies for her husband's Armenian campaign, and in cleverly arranging a basis for a compromise between Antony and Octavianus when all others had failed. The stakes for which Cleopatra played were the secure establishment of her dynasty, the independence of Egypt, and the upbuilding of a great Oriental monarchy in Egypt and Asia. Octavia played to win the Eastern revenues, to save Italy from financial ruin, to protect the Empire from a possible division into two parts, while civil war trembled in the balance. The people of Rome watched the duel between these two women with intense interest. Not only the noble character of Octavia and the indignities put on her appealed to their sympathies, but they felt, as they had in the case of Julia, that peace, prosperity, and the integrity of the Empire were staked upon her success in defeating the wiles of Cleopatra. She failed. Yielding to the entreaties of Cleopatra, in 32 B. C., Antony sent a message to Rome divorcing Octavia, and war followed.

Another woman sacrificed on the altar of politics was Scribonia. Octavianus hastily married her in 40 B. C. to secure an alliance with Sextus Pompeius, who controlled the

Mediterranean, and as precipitately divorced her two years later when he felt prepared to cope with Pompeius.

This constant intermarriage between the families of leading politicians, which is illustrated by the cases of Julia, Octavia, and Scribonia, brought many of these families into blood relationship to one another and went far to make the ruling aristocracy a close corporation. A "new man" had very little chance of election to the consulship if he were pitted against a Metellus or a Cornelius, who could rely not only upon the support of the Metelli or the Cornelii, but also upon the many other powerful families with whom they were allied by marriage. That marriages should be arranged largely on political grounds was a natural development, given the basis upon which the Roman aristocracy rested. This aristocracy was made up of those who held office, or whose ancestors had held office. That fact separated it from the rest of the social world and gave it its exclusiveness. That fact connected it with what was most distinguished in the society and history of the past, and conferred upon it the right to highly prized privileges, insignia, and marks of social distinction. Social and political ambition, therefore, could be gratified by the attainment of one object only, political success, and to this end men and women devoted their most earnest efforts. From this union of society and politics each took its color in large measure, and by it the character of Roman women during the last years of the Republic was profoundly influenced. What the effect of such an alliance is upon politics can be appreciated from a glance at English conditions to-day or from a study of certain periods of French history in which women have played an important rôle behind the scenes in public life. Where such conditions exist, the policy of the government is determined by the salon as well as by the parliament, and political preferment comes largely through social influence. Cæsar's engaging personality, for instance, his dashing manner, and his chivalrous bearing counted largely in his political success. A Marius or a Cincinnatus would have had small chance of winning the prizes in public life. Intrigue is likely to play an important part under such conditions, while revenge and jealousy, personal likes and dislikes will color political aims and methods. A cursory reading of Roman history for the last two decades of the Republic shows the presence of these characteristics in it. They come out clearly, for example, in the brief analysis which has been made of Clodia's share in the politics of her time.

The reflex effect of these conditions on women was equally noteworthy. They made women astute, well-informed, and experienced politicians. Their effect is well shown in the character and career of Servilia. Her antecedents would naturally incline her to the party of reform, since her mother was Livia, sister of Marcus Livius Drusus, the tribune of 91 B. C., who met a violent death because he advocated an increase in the size of the senate and the concession of citizenship to the Italians. With such influences about her in early life, we are not surprised to hear of her in 78 B. C. as the wife of the democratic leader Marcus Junius Brutus, who cast in his lot with Lepidus in the armed revolt against the senate and the Sullan constitution. From this time on for a period of twenty-five years she was actively interested in politics, and no history of this quarter-century is adequate which does not take her into account as a political factor. Her first husband, as we have just noticed, was Marcus Junius Brutus, the radical leader of 78 B. C.; her second husband, Silanus, the democratic consul of 62; her half-brother was Cato of Utica; her lover, Julius Cæsar; while her son and her two sons-in-law were respectively the conspirators, Marcus Brutus, Cassius, and the triumvir Lepidus. In this list we have most of the powerful leaders of the late Republic, and over these men, with the possible exception of her first husband and her brother Cato, she exercised a great influence. We know from the Correspondence of Cicero and from Plutarch that many of the moves which they made were dictated or advised by her. Could we know all the facts Servilia would undoubtedly take her place as one of the most important political figures of the closing years of the Republic. Her influence was always cast with the radicals except during the years immediately following Cæsar's death, when the position of her son Brutus induced her to lend her support to the senatorial party. As the wife of Silanus she made her house a democratic centre. It was here that Cæsar met her. Notoriously fickle as he was in love affairs, he continued in his devotion to her to the end. It was probably her remarkable intellectual qualities, and perhaps her charm of manner, rather than her beauty, which kept him constant. As a mark of his admiration he presented her with a pearl in 59 B. C., which, according to Suetonius, was valued at a quarter of a million dollars. It is significant that this gift was made during the year of Cæsar's first consulship, in which he brought in his first great reform bills and his measures in favor of his two colleagues in the newly formed Triumvirate, Pompey and Crassus. Servilia was in a position to influence Cæsar, therefore, at the very beginning of his active career. That she used it effectively is clear enough from a covert reference in one of Cicero's Letters of this year to a sudden change in Cæsar's policy in the affair of the notorious informer Vettius, a change which, from Cicero's words, we should naturally attribute to Servilia. Cæsar's intimate relations with her probably continued from this time up to his death, and it would be of great interest to know what part of his policy was suggested by her, and how much he owed to her advice and to her social and political influence in carrying it out successfully. Cæsar was a skilful, resourceful politician and did not need the open assistance of Servilia, so that contemporary accounts are silent on this point. But with his death the situation changed. The "liberators," as Cæsar's assassins called themselves, were without purpose or plans. As Cicero says in the light of the murder and of the helplessness of the conspirators after its accomplishment: "Our courage has been that of men; our plans, those of children." The party was without a leader and without organization. Of the conspirators, Decimus Brutus, Cimber, and Trebonius gladly seized the pretext of taking up their provinces to hurry away from Rome. Marcus Brutus and Cassius shut themselves up in their houses in Rome until, from fear of the mob, they thought it wiser to withdraw from the city. Cicero was completely disheartened at the lack of foresight and concerted action which the movements of the conspirators showed, and retired into the country. The republican cause was left without a single leader of weight in the capital. It was this situation, and the danger threatening her son Brutus which forced Servilia to come out openly as one of the leaders of the senatorial party. It must have been a bitter thing for her to join with those who had murdered Cæsar, but her son Brutus was of the number, and that fact constrained her. The tragedy of the situation would be brought home to her still more keenly if Cæsar was the father of Brutus, as some of the ancient writers believed. With Marcus Brutus and Cassius, upon whose military operations in the East the success of the republicans depended, Servilia was in constant communication, and they turned to her so frequently for advice as to exasperate Cicero, who seemed to find her policy too often determined by a desire rather to protect her son than to further the interests of the party. In like manner Cicero thought it incumbent on himself to oppose her vigorously when she tried to prevent the senate from declaring her son-in-law Lepidus a public enemy. It was at her house that a meeting of Cicero and the conspirators who were still in Rome was held, and it was she who directed the deliberations of the gathering and asked each one present to state his view of the situation. She was present, too, at the eventful council of war held at Antium in June, 44 B. C., shortly before the departure of Marcus Brutus and Cassius for the East, and she took a leading part in the discussion there. Her political influence at this time is well shown by the promise which she made on that occasion to bring the senate to repeal one of its decrees to which the conspirators objected. Probably no one of the men present could have made such an undertaking with any hope of success.

This meeting was also attended by her daughter Tertulla and her daughter-in-law Porcia. The marriage of her son to the last-mentioned woman a few years before was a bitter disappointment to Servilia. Porcia was the daughter of Cato, who had been unwearying in his attacks on Cæsar and the other two members of the triumvirate, and the widow of Bibulus, Cæsar's stubborn aristocratic colleague in the consulship of 59 B. C. Porcia was as uncompromising as her father, as devoted to the aristocratic tradition as her first husband, and Servilia viewed with anxiety the influence of such a wife upon the weak and impressionable Brutus. If the latter part of Brutus's career, which is so hard to understand, were analyzed in the light of the influence exerted upon him by Servilia and Porcia, much of his vacillation and inconsistency could be explained. In the years immediately preceding Cæsar's death, the mother and the wife can never have worked in harmony in directing the political action of Brutus, and we can help our understanding of his course by taking into account at one moment the dominance of Servilia, at another, that of Porcia. So, for instance, Brutus's consent to join the conspiracy against Cæsar's life, after receiving so many marks of Cæsar's affection and favor, should be laid, in part at least, to the door of Porcia. Servilia can have had no hand in it, and probably knew nothing of his participation in the enterprise.

It is strange that no writer of fiction has ever thought of making Fulvia his heroine. Ambitious, jealous, cruel, avaricious, and vengeful, she made herself mistress of Rome, and ruled Italy with a capricious tyranny, which surpassed even that of the triumvirs. She married in succession Clodius, Curio, and Antony. To recount their careers is to recite the wildest political excesses of the period of revolution. It was Clodius who for nearly two years held Rome firmly in the grip of his armed bands of desperadoes, overawing the courts and the assemblies and at times even scoffing at the triumvirs and their legions. His career came to an end in a manner befitting such a man. He was killed in a street brawl in 52 B. C. by the faction of Milo, a rival leader. Fulvia married her second husband, Curio, therefore, just before the outbreak of the war between Cæsar and Pompey, when his wild career was at its height. This "most accomplished rake," as Velleius Paterculus styles him, transferred his political allegiance so many times that it is a bewildering task to follow him. His sympathies were first with the bourgeoisie, later he was a conservative, finally a democrat, and in each of his affiliations joined the extreme faction of his party. Shortly after he married Fulvia, Cæsar purchased his services for 100,000 sesterces, as current gossip reported. It was money well spent. For six months during the critical year 50 B. C., Curio single-handed held the senate at bay, and by his clever parliamentary tactics and his appeals to the populace prevented Pompey and the conservatives from carrying through any one of their measures against Cæsar. It was Curio who, according to the current opinion of the times, finally "lighted the torch of war," as Velleius puts it, by inducing Cæsar to cross the Rubicon and advance upon Rome. He was one of the first victims of the war, but Fulvia found a worthy successor to him in Mark Antony. What part she had in spurring Clodius and Curio on to their audacious acts we cannot say, but her course of action after her marriage to her third husband is a matter of history. When Cæsar was struck down, no party and no leader seemed capable of action. The conspirators had looked no further than Cæsar's death, and were without plans. Octavianus, Cæsar's heir, was in Epirus, and Antony, the consul, suspecting further designs on the part of the conspirators, and not knowing their strength, made no move. But this situation of turmoil and confusion was the breath of life to Fulvia. At her instance, Antony took possession of Cæsar's papers, forged documents to suit his own purpose, reorganized the Jacobin clubs, which had served Clodius so well, stirred the populace to indignation at Cæsar's murder, and began the hasty recruiting of troops. It was these measures which forced Brutus, Cassius, and their fellow-conspirators to leave Rome and to abandon Italy to Antony and Fulvia. Her political career reaches its most dramatic point during the months of proscription after the formation of the Second Triumvirate, and after the battle of Philippi in 42 B. C. She rioted in the carnage and confiscation which followed the return of the triumvirs to Rome in 43 B. C., and when the head of Cicero was placed in her hands she pierced with a golden needle the tongue which had scored her first husband Clodius and branded Antony in the Philippics. After 42 B. C. she was practically in control of Italy. She had elevated her brother-in-law Lucius to the consulship, and with his help cowed Octavianus, sowed dissension throughout Italy, and brought the country to the verge of an armed conflict. Only the prompt action of Octavianus's general, Agrippa, in shutting up her adherents in Perusia and reducing that city by a siege, saved Italy from the horrors of another civil war. Thwarted by this reverse in her efforts to precipitate war in Italy, she crossed to Greece with three thousand troops, and, although Antony refused to see her, the bitter feeling which she had stirred up induced him to embark for Italy and lay siege to Brundisium. The war was on in earnest, but at this critical moment Fulvia died, and with her disturbing influence at an end, Antony and Octavianus quickly came to an agreement.

Fulvia typifies the spirit of unrest, disorder, and passion which characterizes the closing years of the Republic as perfectly as Livia, the proud, self-contained, far-seeing, tactful woman whom Octavianus married two years after Fulvia's death, personifies the ideal of the new régime. But Livia belongs to the Empire, not to the Republic, and is outside the limits set for this paper.

ROMAN WOMEN IN THE TRADES AND PROFESSIONS

IN the last paper we attempted to describe the part which Roman women took in politics under the Republic. It was only natural that the tendency which made toward social equality between the sexes, and which had given women a share in the management of public affairs, should in course of time carry them into some of the other vocations which had been reserved for men in the earlier period. Their activity in these masculine fields undoubtedly began under the Republic, but we have scanty means of establishing the fact. Our information on this point comes almost entirely from epitaphs, and the great majority of these are subsequent to republican times.

Let us take up first the three learned professions, medicine, law, and theology. For admission to all of these pursuits modern civilized peoples by law or custom require a preliminar" training and apply some specified test to ascertain the fitness of a candidate. It was not so at Rome. No preliminary training was demanded of those who wished to practise medicine or appear at the bar. So far as theology was concerned, however, the Roman religion was a state religion, and, as among modern peoples where an established church exists, certain conditions of eligibility to the priesthoods were prescribed by ecclesiastical law or immemorial tradition which shut out women from these positions, if priestly offices, like that of Vesta, be excepted, which were open to women only. But new cults were constantly being brought into Italy through the cosmopolitan port of Ostia for which no such traditional prohibition existed, and to priesthoods in many of them women were freely admitted.

Hyginus in his Fabulæ tells us a rather pretty story, which may or may not be true, of the way in which women in the ancient world came to take up the profession of medicine. It seems that in Athens they were forbidden by law to practise medicine, and that in consequence many women died for lack of professional assistance because they were unwilling to consult a male practitioner. Deploring this unfortunate state of affairs a certain Athenian woman, Agnodice by name, cut her hair short, put on the dress of a man, and studied medicine under the distinguished physician, Hierophilus. When she had received the necessary training she offered her services to other women who were in need of them, but her popularity excited the jealousy of other physicians, and on some charge they cited her before the Areopagus. To her judges in the Areopagus she made known her sex; whereupon her medical accusers charged her with violating the law which forbade women to practise medicine. It might have gone hard with her had not the women of Athens hurried to the court, and prevailed upon it to set her free in return for the service which she had rendered them. The law was repealed, and Agnodice, with others who were like-minded, was allowed to pursue the practice of medicine. Agnodice's experience suggests one difficulty which women in ancient times had to encounter, as they do to-day in a measure—the difficulty of securing the requisite training. Upon this point, however, it may be said, that medicine was not so highly developed an art in Athens or in Rome as it is with us; and although there were some very skilful physicians, the standard set for the average practitioner was not a high one. Then, too, as soon as the social prejudice which prevented women from entering the professions had broken down, distinguished physicians in Rome do not seem to have been unwilling to take women as their pupils. At all events, a certain Restituta expresses her gratitude in an honorary inscription to the emperor's physician who had instructed her in medicine. Women physicians were freely recognized in the law even, for the Code of Justinian refers to "physicians of either sex."

That the practice of medicine by women in the second century of our era was fairly common seems to be clear from the fact that Soranus, a writer of that century, in treating of the maladies of women, discusses the qualifications which women who take up this branch of medicine must have. Among other things, he says they must know how to write; they must have a good memory, robust health, and an even temperament. They must be familiar with dietetics, pharmacy, and ordinary surgery. In particular he urges discretion, "for the affairs of the household and the life secrets of every one will be intrusted to you." Still, if we may judge from sepulchral inscriptions, the number of women who practised medicine in the Empire was comparatively small. Probably not more than one in ten of the physicians whose names appear in the Latin epitaphs were women. Some of them, however, won distinction in their profession. Theodorus Priscianus, a court physician of the fifth century, A. D., dedicated the third book of his medical treatise to a woman physician, and a certain Scantia Redempta is celebrated in her epitaph as "a leader in the science of medicine."

The story of Agnodice, given above, may be simply an ætiological myth invented to explain how women came to practise medicine, and to account for the fact that they confined their practice to patients of their own sex. No women are described on gravestones as surgeons or aurists, and among many extant stamps of oculists no one bears the name of a woman. Some women have a title which might indicate that they were general practitioners, but probably even they devoted themselves to obstetrics, massage, and the preparation of cosmetics, the art of the "beauty-doctor," and nervous ailments, specialties which are frequently mentioned in literature and the inscriptions. In taking up the last-mentioned specialty they must have found plenty of patients. The luxurious tastes of the late Republic and the early Empire, constant travelling to and fro, the exactions of fashionable life in the capital and at villas on the sea-shore and in the mountains, and the many public performances which great crowds attended at the theatre and the arena furnished the best possible conditions for the development of nervous diseases, among women especially. The lack of balance and self-restraint on the part of the Roman women of this period, which the poets satirize unsparingly, would indicate the prevalence of these disorders, even if Martial did not now and then refer to the *hystericæ* and their treatment by women physicians. That in treating such cases women physicians sometimes employed other remedies than those included in the pharmacopœia is suggested by the advice which Soranus gives them, speaking as the conventional practitioner, not to resort to superstitious methods. We are not surprised to find that the sick often turned to religion for help in their physical ailments. Several cures by faith are recorded in the monuments. In one case a story is told in the inscriptions which furnishes a curious parallel to experiences reported from time to time by converts to our present-day methods of religious healing. A certain Felix records the fact on a dedicatory stone in very ungrammatical, but vigorous Latin that "after having been given up by his physicians his sight had been restored through the kindness of the goddess Bona Dea and the medical treatment of her priestess Caunia Fortunata." Felix's experience with physicians reminds one of the remarks of the freedman Seleucus at the famous dinner of Trimalchio, that "a doctor is nothing else than a sort of consolation to the mind."

The medical profession was not one into which women of the better class entered. The art was introduced into Italy from Greece and almost all the men who followed it were Greek freedmen. An examination of the names on tombstones shows us that the women also who practised medicine were of the same nationality and of the same low social standing.

So far as the legal profession is concerned, no technical training was required of those who wished to enter it, but the law did not recognize the right of women to appear as advocates. It is a little surprising, after having secured the recognition of their independence before the law, and after having gained admission to almost all the vocations previously monopolized by men, that they failed to carry this masculine stronghold. Apparently they made some progress toward winning the privilege, since we find a provision in the Praetorian Edict of Ulpian forbidding them to appear as advocates. Such a prohibition would scarcely have been made if women had not attempted to practise law. However, in certain circumstances, women might appear in court in their own defence. That gossipy writer Valerius Maximus mentions two such instances of women who argued their own cases. His opinion of the propriety of their action may be easily inferred from his remark in introducing the cases: "One must mention even those women upon whom nature and the modesty which befits the *stola* was not strong enough to impose silence in the forum and in the courts." One of the two, he tells us, because she pleaded her own cause as a man would have done, was dubbed "the Man-woman," Androgyne. Of the other, who argued her case before the praetor, "not because there was a lack of advocates, but because she was filled with presumption," he says, "she lived to the second consulship of Gaius Cæsar, and the first of Publius Servilius, for one ought to record the time when such an abnormal being died rather than when she was born."

The anthropomorphic element entered in large measure into the religion of the Romans, and it was only natural that the family relations should be reflected in their religious conceptions. Thus, corresponding to the husband and wife in this world, were Jupiter and Juno in the celestial world, Janus and Vesta, Sol and Luna, Minerva and Mars, Pluto and Proserpina, and the temples of the two members of each sacred pair were often in close proximity to each other; and as men had charge of the rites of Jupiter, for instance, so women took a leading part in the cult of Juno. In fact, the differentiation of the conception of Juno from that of Jupiter, and the development of her cult, would almost seem to have run parallel to the acquisition of individuality by woman and to her escape from the control of her husband.

Perhaps women have always taken a more intense interest in religious matters than men. It seems to have been so in Rome. It is interesting, for instance, to note that the earliest Latin document of any length which we have is a decree of the senate from 186 B. C. directed particularly against the excesses into which women had run in carrying on the rites of Bacchus. Even the severe repressive measures which this statute provided do not seem to have been effectual, for very recently utensils connected with the cult of Bacchus have been found in a Roman house which is as late as the first century B. C. Many of the priesthoods were held by them from the earliest times. The cult of Vesta was, of course, entirely in their hands, to say nothing of the predominant part which they had in conducting the rites of Ceres and other female deities. The wives of many priests, too, held an official position recognized by the state, and a great many tombstones are to be found throughout the Empire in honor of the *flaminica* who participated with the *flamen* in directing the combined cults of the Goddess Rome and of Augustus.

From discussing the three learned professions one naturally passes to the pursuit of literature. The indirect influence of women upon Latin literature under the Empire must have been very great. Even if there were no specific proofs of this fact, we could draw the inference from the literary conditions of to-day. It is freely stated in some quarters, for instance, that the character of the present-day drama is determined by women. It seems to be true, at all events, that the playwright and the theatrical manager must make sure of pleasing them, if the theatres are to be filled. The novel was invented to please women, and, since they make up the majority of the novel-readers, the novelist must be guided by their taste in the matter of fiction. At Rome, even as early as the time of Horace, we hear of the drawing-room critic surrounded by his "lady pupils," and Juvenal's famous diatribe against the literary woman a century later will be recalled. "Yet *she* is more offensive," he says, "who, as soon as she has taken her place at the table, praises Virgil, excuses the doomed Dido, matches and pairs off the poets, then weighs in the balance Virgil on the one side, Homer on the other. Grammarians yield; teachers of rhetoric are vanquished; the entire company is silent; not even a lawyer, a public crier, nor any other woman even may speak. . . . Let not the matron who is joined to you in marriage be the mistress of a style, or evolve an argument with well-rounded speech, and let her not know all the histories, but some things there are in books which I would have her not understand. I hate the woman who is always turning back to the grammatical rules of Palæmon and consulting them, always following the law and the rationale of speech; the feminine antiquary who recalls verses unknown to me, and corrects the words of an unpolished friend which even a man would not observe. Let a husband be allowed to make a solecism. The wise person puts a limit even on things good in themselves." It was the drawing-room literature written to please women of this type upon which Persius pours his scorn in his first satire — literature cast in an archaistic, pedantic style, with well-rounded periods and sonorous words. If we should stop to ask ourselves what literary productions we owe to the inspiration which individual women gave the Roman poets we should recall such women as the Lesbia of Catullus, the Cynthia of Propertius, and the Delia of Tibullus; but with the indirect influence which womankind exerted upon literature, or with the inspiration which the Latin poets found in the beauty or the accomplishments of individual women, we are not concerned here. Our purpose is a much more modest one, to get some idea of the extent to which women entered the literary field.

It was only natural that among the many women interested in literature some should try their hand at composition. Fate has not been kind to those of their number who courted the Muses. In most cases they are names only to us. Few of their productions have come down to modern times, and we must judge of their quality mainly from the passing comments made upon them by contemporary writers of the masculine sex. We have said that fate was unkind to them. Perhaps she was kinder to them than we think. The bits which are extant and what we are told by the ancients of the literary work of women do not fill us with regret at our loss. Very few, if any of them, made literature their profession, as Horace did, for instance. Almost all of them were dilettanti, or else the pursuit of literature was quite incidental to other interests. So far as form was concerned, they showed a marked preference for verse, although, as we shall see, at least three of the most noteworthy pieces of literary work done by women were in prose. It would be interesting to speculate upon the schools to which these literary women belonged, and upon the literary movements which they followed, but it would be largely speculation, not based on full and trustworthy information.

The most noteworthy literary women among the Romans were Cornelia, Sulpicia, Agrippina the Younger, and the author of a Pilgrimage to the Holy Land. Cornelia is the first woman of whose literary activity we have any record. She was the first woman, too, it will be remembered, to make her influence felt on Roman public life. All that we have left from her pen are extracts from two letters (or two extracts from the same letter) addressed to her son Gaius. They were written after the death of Tiberius and deal with a subject near to her heart, the punishment of his enemies, and the execution of his political plans. Some fifty years ago their authenticity was called in question. But no one doubts it to-day. The sternness of their tone, and the quaintness of their diction, and their manner, which is rather spirited than logical in the masculine way, bespeak the daughter of Scipio and the mother of the Gracchi. The opinion was hazarded in the last paper that Gaius was led by his mother's teachings to take up the work of Tiberius where his brother dropped it at his death. These letters to Gaius furnish strong confirmation of that view.

Sulpicia belonged to the literary circle of Messalla, of which Tibullus was the most distinguished member. She has left us a half-dozen elegies celebrating her love for a young Greek named Cerinthus. They are all short poems of eight lines or less, graceful in form and sincere in tone. Their authenticity has been questioned, but apparently without good reason.

In the fourth book of his Annals Tacitus gives us an account of an interview between the Emperor Tiberius and Agrippina the Elder, the wife of Germanicus, the emperor's hated rival. The story of this meeting Tacitus says he has taken from the Memoirs of the younger Agrippina. Unfortunately Agrippina's work has not come down to us. It would be hard to think of a document of livelier interest for the reigns of Tiberius, Claudius, and perhaps Nero, than the reminiscences of the woman whose mother knew the ins and outs of politics under Tiberius, and who was herself the wife of Claudius and the mother of Nero. We might hear something of the wiles by which she led Claudius to marry her, and to pass over his own son and make her son by a former marriage heir to the throne. Agrippina might throw some light upon her offensive and defensive alliance with Pallas, and her political duel with the clever freedman Narcissus, upon her regency during the early part of Nero's reign, and her gradual loss of influence over him. Could we make a guess from reading her book whether she really poisoned her husband Claudius or not? Even if she did not let us into the secrets of these political intrigues, in an age like this of ours, when autobiography is the popular form of literature, when curiosity concerning the private life of distinguished people knows no bounds, any sketches of court scenes in her day or any stories of the intimate life of Tiberius, Claudius, or Nero would be read with avidity. Is it possible that Tacitus drew from these Memoirs part of the material upon which he bases his estimate of Tiberius, and that we owe to Agrippina the repellent picture which he has painted of that emperor?

The most noteworthy find in the field of Latin literature during the last twenty years was the discovery in a library at Arezzo, Italy, of a manuscript containing an account of the pilgrimage of a certain woman to the Holy Land. This holy lady made a journey to Palestine in the fourth century of our era from her home, somewhere in western Europe, and she has left us a record of her impressions and adventures. It is the longest extant piece of Latin literature from a feminine hand. The document has not come down to us in a complete form, so that we cannot learn from it the name of the author. Many scholars have held the opinion, however, that it is the work of a certain Silvia, the sister of Rufinus, a Roman prefect of the fourth century. This identification depends in part on the extraordinary powers of endurance which the writer had in climbing mountains, in making long journeys on foot, in putting up with heat and cold, and in the contempt which she showed for the comforts and conveniences of life. These characteristics harmonize perfectly with the austere vigor of the holy pilgrim Silvia, to whom other qualities of the book point, and of whom Bishop Palladius relates this incident: On coming in her travels to Pelusium in Egypt, she found that the deacon Jubinus, who had been stricken with fever, had bathed in cold water and then laid down to rest. When Silvia saw him, she reproved him for his weakness, saying to him: "Yield not, yield not; look at me; I am in my sixtieth year, and water has touched no part of my body even when divers maladies have come upon me, except the tips of my fingers before communion, . . . and when sick I have not reclined upon a couch nor been carried in a lectica." Very lately it has been urged with considerable probability that the Pilgrimage was really written by Aetheria, a Spanish abbess. Whether she or Silvia was the author matters little to us. At all events the book was the work of a woman. The writer had evidently had no previous experience in literary composition; her vocabulary is very limited, and her style monotonous and repetitious. But as a woman's straightforward record of her experiences while making a long and difficult journey through Egypt, Palestine, and Mesopotamia, and of the impressions which the sacred places in the Holy Land made upon her, the book has a lively interest for us. To one who is interested in church ceremonial and Palestinian topography it is of course of peculiar value, while to the student of language it is a mine of information, because the author had no training in formal literary Latin, but wrote in the popular Latin which she used in conversation. The brief sketches which have been given of the writings of Cornelia, Sulpicia, Agrippina, and Sancta Silvia, or Aetheria, show pretty clearly that women made no important contributions to Latin literature.

In the good old days of the legitimate drama under Plautus, Terence, Accius, and Pacuvius women never appeared upon the stage. Feminine rôles were taken by men in female dress. But with the appearance of the mime and the farce in the first century before our era, women began to take part in theatrical and musical performances. Their larger participation in such matters under the

Empire is proved by the discovery of the burying place of a guild of women mimes, just outside Rome, along one of the highways leading from the city. Women took a very active part in public musical performances, if we may draw an inference from the number of epitaphs which we find in honor of women who had been solo singers and flute players. One young woman named Eucharis, in a very pretty metrical epitaph of twenty-two lines, which probably dates from the first century before our era, claims the credit of having introduced the musical monologue on the Roman stage. Yet no women performers ever attained the high degree of popular favor which was reached by Apelles the musical virtuoso under Caligula, Menecrates the composer under Nero, or Paris the mime whom Martial has immortalized in one of his epigrams:

> Thou that beatest the Flaminian Way,
> Pass not this noble tomb, but stay;
> Here Rome's delight, and Nile's salt treasure,
> Art, graces, sport, and sweetest pleasure,
> The grief and glory of the stage,
> And all the Cupids of the age,
> And all the Venuses, lie here,
> Interr'd in Paris' sepulchre.

Most of the women who went on the stage were of Greek extraction, as their names indicate, and belonged to the lower classes.

The same thing is true of the women who engaged in trade or handiwork. Passing over those, like nurses and maids, who were employed in household service, and noticing only the women who took up occupations which brought them into contact with the public, we find mentioned in the inscriptions costumers, seamstresses, washerwomen, weavers, women in charge of estates, fish-mongers, and barmaids. Their commonest occupations were the various trades connected with the making and repairing of clothing. Very likely the epitaphs do not give us a correct idea of the number of Roman women engaged in business. Probably in ancient Rome, as in modern Rome or in Paris, the tradesman's or artisan's wife helped him to keep his shop, but that fact naturally finds no place on a tombstone. Most of the women in this category, as we have noticed above, were freedwomen, but the women who were engaged in one branch of business at Rome belonged to the most exclusive circles of Roman society. The trade in question was the brick business, an industry which was largely controlled by women, and by women of the leading families. This fact is evident from the stamp, found on almost every Roman brick, indicating the brickkiln or the estate from which the brick comes. Some of the stamps bear the names of such distinguished women as the Empress Plotina, Arria Fadilla, mother of Antoninus Pius, and Faustina, the consort of Marcus Aurelius; but the names which occur most frequently are those of Domitia Lucilla the Elder and her daughter, who apparently had the leading brick business in Rome for half a century.

If we make a general survey of the facts which have been noted above, it is clear that Roman women took an active part in the literary and religious life of the time, and in many of the cults held priesthoods or officially recognized positions from very early times. Their interest in literature, however, was not serious, and they have produced very little of permanent value. In the practice of law they never succeeded in getting a sure foothold. Women of the lower classes entered freely into the medical profession and the trades, but so far as medicine is concerned women confined their practice to members of their own sex. The principal branches of business which they took up were those connected with the manufacture of wearing apparel. The pursuits of the shopkeeper and the artisan were naturally left to the lower classes, but women of standing in society engaged in industries organized on a large scale, as we can see clearly enough in the case of the brick business.

THE THEATRE AS A FACTOR IN ROMAN POLITICS UNDER THE REPUBLIC

IN our day political opinion finds expression or enthusiasm for a cause, or a candidate is stimulated, through the public press, on the platform with its accessories in the way of processions and receptions, and at the elections. In Rome under the Republic the two last-mentioned methods of testing popular sentiment are to be found, but the place which the press holds with us as an organ for the expression of public opinion on political matters seems to have been taken by the theatre, for, as Cicero says in his oration for Sestius, "in three places especially the judgment and desire of the Roman people can be made known, viz., at the *contio* [or gatherings for public discussion], at the *comitia* [or meetings of the popular assemblies], and when the people come together at the games and the gladiatorial contests." [1] He then proceeds to discuss at some length,[2] in the subsequent chapters of his oration, the attitude of the people in their public meetings, at the ballot-box, and at the plays and games, and comes to the conclusion [3] that public opinion found true expression only at the theatrical performances and the gladiatorial contests. Was this true? Was the theatre such an important political factor and the only correct index of public feeling in Cicero's day? His conclusion cannot be accepted without question, because he is not an unprejudiced judge of the matter. The demonstrations in the theatre and at the games during the period of his exile, of which he is speaking here, had favored him, but the *contiones* and the *comitia* of that year had been hostile to him. This situation might account for his view that the real sentiments of the people were best indicated in the theatre. It is worth while considering the correctness of his statement by examining very briefly the condition of the *contiones* and *comitia* under the late Re-

[1] Cicero, *pro Sestio*, 106. Some of the passages cited in this paper might not be entirely clear apart from the context in which they stand, so that I have thought it wise to give them in translation and in such an English form as will bring out the points of interest to us. [2] *Ibid.*, 106–127. [3] *Ibid.*, 127.

public, and by glancing at the part which the theatre played in political life. A complete presentation of all the evidence would be out of place here, nor is it necessary for our purpose.

It is convenient to approach the subject from the negative side and to ask, first, if Cicero's low estimate of the political organizations of his day is correct. On this point there can be little doubt. The city of Rome grew at a tremendous rate during the first century B. C., and most of the new-comers were men of little worth. They were discouraged and bankrupt farmers; free laborers, who were driven out of the country districts by slavery; ne'er-do-weels, who wished to live upon the largess of the state; men attracted to Rome by the theatre, the games, and the other amusements and excitements which the city had to offer; people who preferred to live by their wits rather than by the labor of their hands, and found a more promising field in Rome for the exercise of their talents than the small towns and the country offered; the veterans, whose long terms of service in the field had made it well-nigh impossible for them to take up contentedly or successfully the humdrum life of a farmer or artisan; and, finally, the hordes of freedmen who had low standards of political honor and little sympathy with Roman political traditions. All these people had the right to the suffrage, and their vote was a salable article of considerable value. They naturally attached themselves to some political leader; they were organized into companies, and cast their votes as they were instructed. From meetings of the popular assemblies made up largely of such elements one could hardly expect an honest expression of opinion. The low moral character of the electoral and legislative bodies was not the only charge to be made against them. They were centres of chicanery and turbulence. One sees the consul Metellus slipping into the Campus by a roundabout route to prevent a political opponent from postponing a meeting of the assembly by announcing that the auspices were unfavorable,[1] or Milo anticipating the other party by occupying the Campus with an armed force at midnight on the day before the election, and holding it until noon against the opposite side, "to the unbounded delight of everybody and to his own great credit,"

[1] Cic. *ad Att.* iv, 3, 4.

as Cicero, whose political sympathies favored Milo, regards the manœuvre. Or sometimes political workers block up the approaches to the ballot-boxes or see to it that ballots of one kind only are supplied to the voters.[1] The honesty of elections was vitiated still more flagrantly by the use of force. For this purpose bands of retainers were organized and drilled,[2] and by their use the *comitia* were overawed and peaceable citizens were kept away from the meetings. The illegal employment of money was even more fatal to honest elections than the use of force. Probably bribery has never been so prevalent as it was during the last century of the Republic. To this fact the bribery laws of 67, 63, 55, and 52 B. C., with their increasing penalties and ingenious devices for securing evidence, abundantly testify.[3] The buying of votes was reduced to a system. The baser citizens were formed into political clubs, and professional agents were employed in organizing and paying venal voters. The use of money was carried to such an extent in 54 B. C., for instance, that every one of the candidates for the con-

[1] *Ibid.*, i, 14, 5.
[2] Cic. *pro Sest.* 34; *ad Att.* i, 13, 3.
[3] Cic. *ad Att.* i, 16, 13.

sulship in that year was indicted for bribery.[1]

The state of the *contiones* for the discussion of public questions was still worse. Here the test of citizenship was not applied, and the meetings were packed with freedmen and slaves[2] whose *clamor contionalis* became a byword. Companies of bravoes were organized,[3] who drowned the voice of a hostile speaker, drove him from the rostra, or converted the place of meeting into a veritable shambles.[4] A frequent concomitant of these public meetings was a demonstration in the streets. Thus, Cicero tells us[5] that Cæsar tried to lead the mob from the *contio* to surround the house of Bibulus, and during the scarcity of grain Clodius induced his audience to march through the streets and threaten the senate.[6] The counterpart to these outbursts of popular passion was furnished by the street demonstrations in honor of a political leader. Sometimes they were of an impromptu character, like the gathering of the great company which escorted Cicero home when he

[1] Cic. *ad Q. fr.* iii, 2, 3; *ad Att.* iv, 17, 2.
[2] Cic. *ad Att.* ii, 1, 8; ii, 16, 1.
[3] Cic. *pro Sest.* 34.
[4] Cic. *ad Q. fr.* ii, 3, 2–4; *Ibid.*, i, 2, 15; *pro Sest.* 77.
[5] Cic. *ad Att.* ii, 21, 5.
[6] *Ibid.*, iv, 1, 6.

laid down the office of consul, or like the ovation which he received on returning from exile;[1] or they were carefully prepared, like the organized escorts of honor upon which so much stress is laid in the little pamphlet on Candidacy for the Consulship. All these facts fully substantiate Cicero's statement that the opinion of the Roman people on political matters did not find free and honest expression in an ordinary meeting of the *contio* or *comitia*.

Is the rest of his assertion equally trustworthy? Was the theatre a political factor to be reckoned with, and did it indicate the real course of the political current? In the theatre the sentiment of the people was indicated on occasions of two sorts, either when a political leader entered, or when a passage in a play applied, or was thought to apply, to a local situation. We have several interesting reports of cases where demonstrations of the first kind occurred. For instance, the popularity of Curio's course in 59 B. C. was clearly shown by the enthusiasm which his coming into the theatre aroused,[2] whereas the faint applause with which Cæsar was received[3] when he entered was so significant of the

[1] *Ibid.*, 4, 1. [2] *Ibid.* ii, 18, 1. [3] *Ibid.*, 19, 3.

attitude of the people that it created great anxiety in the democratic party, of which he was a leader, and in the opinion of the conservative Cicero was likely to bring about a political reaction, and this in spite of the fact that Cæsar controlled the *contiones* and *comitia*. How Hortensius was received after having taken an unpopular course in a notorious political trial Cælius cleverly describes, by applying to the roar of disapproval of the great throng in the theatre when Hortensius entered, and their derisive whistling, an onomatopoetic line from the famous storm passage in Pacuvius,

> "The rumbling, roaring, rolling thunder, and the whistling of the cordage,"

and he adds this comment: "This was the more noticed, because Hortensius had reached old age unassailed by hisses; but on that occasion he was roundly enough hissed to satisfy any man his life long, and to make Hortensius regret at last his victory at the trial." [1] Bribery and the use of force, which made political meetings and elections an untrustworthy indication of the sentiment of the

[1] Cic. *ad. fam.* viii, 2, 1.

people, could not be used with equal success in the theatre. Honest and peaceable citizens could be kept away from the *contiones* and *comitia*, but no Roman would give up the high privilege of seeing the play. Bands of hired political supporters might try to give their employer an enthusiastic welcome and to convey the impression that an unpopular leader had the support of the citizens, but their applause would be drowned by the hisses of the great mass of the people, or would pale into insignificance before the enthusiasm aroused by the entrance of the leader of the opposite party. Under the Empire, even after public meetings had been given up and the *comitia* had disappeared, the public clung to their right of expressing in the theatre or at the games their approval or disapproval of the conduct of the emperor.

More interesting still were references from the stage to contemporary persons or events. Sometimes the playwright himself introduced the reference, sometimes the actor applied to the local situation a passage which in the play as it came from the pen of the playwright had no such significance. In proportion as it kept itself free from Hellenizing influences, the lighter forms of the national drama would seem always to have referred to contemporary affairs with considerable freedom. The attitude of Nævius, the first great writer of comedy, is clearly indicated in a passage in the Agitatoria, "Freedom (of speech) I have always esteemed more highly than money and held as much to be preferred to it";[1] and the following defiant sentiment he puts into the mouth of the people, "Against that of which I have approved in the theatre no tyrant dare transgress."[2] These statements and other bold ones to be found elsewhere in the extant fragments of his comedies,[3] the story of his imprisonment for his freedom in criticising men and things,[4] as given by Gellius, and the epigram upon him which emphasizes his "Campanian[5] boldness," show clearly enough the freedom with which he spoke of prominent men and events of his own time, even if his daring fling at the scandal connected with Scipio's birth,[6] and his bold hint that the Metelli owed the consulship to good luck rather than to personal merit,[7] had not come down to us. Plautus

[1] Ribbeck, *Com. Rom. Fr.*, Naev. 9–10.
[2] *Ibid.*, Naev. 72–73.
[3] *Ibid.*, Naev. 20, 111–112.
[4] Gellius, iii, 3, 15.
[5] *Ibid.*, i, 24, 1.
[6] Ribbeck, Naev. 108–110.
[7] Ps. Ascon. p. 140, ed. Or.

refers frequently to general conditions in his own time, but, either warned by the fate of Nævius, or in obedience to the tendency which becomes more and more apparent in Cæcilius and Terence, says little or nothing which could give offence to specific individuals. Whether references were made to political affairs in plays like the *togatae*, where the scene and the coloring were Roman rather than Greek, it is difficult to say, because of the scanty fragments which we have of this form of the drama; but that they were a characteristic feature of another form of dramatic entertainment, the mime, seems to be clear from the famous passage at arms between the actors and playwrights, Laberius and Syrus,[1] and from Cicero's mock anxiety lest Laberius make his friend Trebatius, who was campaigning with Cæsar in Gaul, the hero of one of his farces. An interesting passage in one of Cicero's letters from 44 B. C.[2] shows what an important political factor the mime was. Cicero remarks to Atticus: "I received two letters from you yesterday. From the first one I learned about the theatre and Publilius [Syrus

[1] Macrob. *Sat* ii, 7.
[2] Cic. *ad Att.* xiv, 2, 1; *ad fam.* xii, 2, 2.

the playwright] — encouraging indications of a united populace. The applause, in fact, given to Lucius Cassius seemed to me at any rate a delicate compliment." That writers of mimes occupied themselves with political matters may be inferred also from other statements in the Letters of Cicero. In one of these he hints at passages descriptive of Cæsar's exploits in the plays which Laberius and Publilius Syrus brought out at the dramatic festival given by the dictator to celebrate his victory at Thapsus. Speaking of his own philosophical acceptance of the political situation, he says, "In fact, I have already become so callous, that at the games given by our friend Cæsar, with perfect equanimity I gazed upon Titus Plancus and listened to the productions of Laberius and Publilius."[1] In another letter he remarks to Atticus, "You will write to me if you have anything of practical importance; if not, describe to me fully the attitude of the people [in the theatre] and the local hits in the mimes."[2]

We have noticed that all the extant passages in which playwrights refer to contemporary politics are to be found in the lighter forms

[1] Cic. *ad fam.* xii, 18, 2.

[2] Cic. *ad Att.* xiv, 3, 2.

of the drama. On the other hand, the verses which actors apply to politicians or public events of their own time occur mainly in tragedy. How frequently lines were applied in this way and how quick the audience was to see their application is clear from a passage in Cicero's oration in defence of Sestius, "Not to pass over even this point, among the many and varied utterances [on the stage] there has never been a passage in which some sentiment expressed by a poet seemed to apply to our own time, which either escaped the whole audience or which the actor himself did not bring out." [1] An illustration of the alertness of the people in this respect is furnished by an incident mentioned in the same connection.[2] The Andromacha Aechmalotis of Ennius was being given, and when the passage "I have seen it all enveloped in flames," which describes the burning of Priam's palace, was reached, the actor and the audience applied it to the destruction of Cicero's house by Clodius, and the people burst into tears at the thought of the wrong done their great leader. The passage from Accius,[3] "You permit him to be an exile; you allow him to be driven out;

[1] Cic. *pro Sest.* 118. [2] *Ibid.*, 121. [3] *Ibid.*, 122.

you put up with his banishment," brought to the dullest mind the picture of the exile in Thessalonica, while "Tullius, who had been the bulwark of the liberty of the citizens," was encored again and again; and when, in giving the Simulans of Afranius, the entire company of actors turned toward the place where Clodius sat and thundered at him the lines, "This, O foul, base man, is the outcome and conclusion of the life of a libertine,"[1] even that stormy petrel of politics was aghast at the probable effect of the incident on popular sentiment. Pompey felt the same anxiety at the Festival of Apollo in 59 B. C., when the tragedian Diphilus applied to him some lines from a play in which he was acting,[2] and Pacuvius's line, "To think that I have saved them that they might destroy me," which Cæsar's followers, after his death, put in the mouth of their leader, probably played no small rôle in arousing the wrath of the people against the conspirators.[3] Now and then a player who found he had struck a popular chord followed up his success by improvising a line, as an actor in a play of Accius did on a certain occasion.[4]

[1] Cic. *pro Sest.* 123.
[2] Cic. *ad Att.* ii, 19, 3.
[3] Suet. *Iul.* 84.
[4] Cic. *pro Sest.* 121.

A study of the theatre as a political factor under the Empire lies outside the scope of this paper, but the theatre or circus continued to furnish almost the only means which the great mass of the people had for expressing their opinion on public men or public questions.[1]

[1] Suet. *Aug.* 53; *Tib.* 45; *Nero*, 39; *Galba*, 13.

PETRONIUS: A STUDY IN ANCIENT REALISM

THE Latin novelist, Petronius, of the first century of our era, has been strangely neglected, as it seems to me. In our latest, and in other respects our best, history of the early novel even his name is not mentioned. It is a perilous thing to discuss the work of an author whose life and writings are so little known to the general public; and when even the professional student of literary history ignores his existence, it is like flying in the face of Providence. But the important position which Petronius holds as the creator of a new *genre* of literature may properly justify the imprudence. Furthermore the small circle of his admirers is likely to be enlarged in the near future, since two good translations into English of a portion of his work have lately appeared, and he may at last be rescued from the obscurity in which he languishes.

Perhaps it is not quite correct to say that the facts in the life of Petronius are not widely known to-day. Whoever has read the "Quo Vadis," of Sienkiewicz, his great Polish follower in the field of prose fiction, will know what manner of man Petronius was, and many of us who remember the incident where the hero of Quo Vadis purchases at the book shop of Avirnus a copy of his Satyricon for a friend, Vinicius, bidding him keep the author's name a secret, may wonder whether the book has survived the wreck of the Roman Empire, and, if it has, what its character and value are. A part of it has come down to us, perhaps a fourth or fifth of the entire work. In subject and in treatment it is exactly such a production as one would expect from the pen of a man like Petronius. The reader will remember in the novel of Sienkiewicz the closing hours of the life of Petronius. The description is founded upon fact, for it is based upon the pages of the historian Tacitus. After holding securely for a long time the unique position of director-in-chief of the imperial pleasures under the capricious voluptuary, Nero, Petronius at last saw another supplant him in the emperor's favor. Knowing that his days were numbered, he decided not to wait for the inevitable sentence of death, but, inviting his friends to dinner, he opened one or more of his veins and passed away in the enjoyment of those pleasures to which he had given so many years of his life; and it was characteristic of the man that he bound up the wounds when the conversation took a turn which interested him, and that, as Tacitus tells us, he did not pass these last hours in discoursing on the immortality of the soul and the teachings of the sages, but in listening to the recital of gay and trifling verses. This is the only information of present interest which the ancients have left us concerning the great Roman realist. Perhaps it would help us to a more intelligent understanding of his work, to sketch in somewhat fully, as a background to this impressionist view of Petronius, which Tacitus gives us, a picture of the times in which he lived; but a few words must suffice upon this point.

In the period of one hundred years which intervened between the middle of the first century B. C. and the middle of the first century A. D. Roman life and character had undergone tremendous changes of a social, political, and religious nature. The beginning of this period is distinguished by the completion of

Pompey's conquests in the East, and the consequent influx into Italy of thousands of Greeks and Orientals, who brought with them, to undermine the comparatively simple life of the Roman, the standards of luxury of the ancient and effete civilizations. Many of the newcomers were slaves, and the cheapness of their labor soon drove the peasant proprietors from the country districts of Italy to Rome, to swell the number of idle men already in the metropolis. The Romans were quick also to appreciate the opportunities which the Orient offered them for making fortunes, and the Eastern provinces were soon filled with Roman tax-gatherers, traders, and bankers, who came back ultimately to spend their money in Italy with all the prodigality which the exaggerated Oriental ideas of luxury could develop in parvenus. Political changes at home and abroad in this period were almost as marked as economic changes. The brain and brawn of every citizen had been needed in the early struggles of Rome for existence, and in her later contests for supremacy with rivals like Carthage. But at the beginning of our era Rome's enemies abroad were not to be feared, and the men who protected her far-away frontiers were no longer the citizens who left the field and the bench, to return to them later with the addition of those forceful qualities which come from military discipline, but professional soldiers who passed their lives in the provinces. In civil life the emperor had gained so complete a mastery that there was no longer any outlet for the political ambition of the man of genius, nor any opportunity for the average citizen to gratify his natural desire for a part in the control of affairs. A religion with a strong spiritual or moral tendency like Judaism might have stemmed the tide setting toward selfishness and materialism, but, as a writer upon morals has remarked, "the Roman religion, though in its best days an admirable system of moral discipline, was never an independent source of moral enthusiasm." In the period which we are considering the Roman had outgrown his religion.

The extension of his horizon, and an acquaintance with more highly developed religious and philosophical systems had shown him the narrowness and puerility of his own faith, and as yet nothing had come to take its place. As a result of the social conditions which developed out of these changes men's thoughts were turned in upon themselves, and their lives were given over to the gratification of their personal tastes. The literature of the period reflected the temper of the times, as a literature always does. The age of heroic achievement which could furnish an inspiration to lofty flights of the Muse was past. The labored efforts of Lucan in writing an epic on the civil war, and the artificial tragedies of Seneca, illustrate this fact for the generation of Petronius, if any illustration is needed. It was a period of introspection, when each man's thoughts were limited to himself and those about him, when he had no share and no interest in the greater concerns of politics or religion or philosophy. The realistic romance dealing with the affairs of everyday life is the natural product of such a state of society, and it was in such circumstances that the great realistic novel of Petronius, which is also, I think, the earliest-known romance of any sort, saw the light of day. It is a significant fact that prose fiction made its appearance after every other independent form of literature in prose and verse had come into existence and lived its life, so to speak. The same statement may be made of the development of romance among the Greeks and in modern times. Prose fiction always seems to spring up in an imitative rather than in a creative literary period. As I have already said, only a portion of the work of Petronius is extant, but even the part left us forms an invaluable contribution to the literature of prose fiction, and furnishes a striking proof of the genius of its author.

The action of the story in its complete form, as the contemporaries of Petronius had it, took place in certain Italian and provincial towns. Three principal episodes of considerable length have come down to us, and in them the scene is laid in two Italian towns. Some one has said that our own novelist Howells was the first writer to reproduce accurately the local color of different towns within the borders of the same country. I am afraid that Howells's supporters must yield to Petronius his claim to this distinction. When one follows the hero in the novel of Petronius from the shores of the Bay of Naples, where the scene is at first laid, to Croton, in Southern Italy, he comes into an entirely different atmosphere. He passes out of the circle of Rome's influence. The provincial aristocracy of the little Campanian village, making its crude attempts to imitate the manners of the metropolis, gives place to the elegant depravity of a town which was essentially Greek in its mode of life; and the differences which existed between the two types of society are presented in so subtle a fashion that even a close student, like Zola, of the characteristics which society of the same grade shows in different modern cities might admire the result. The hero of the romance is a Greek freedman who lives by his wits. Gathered about him in the story is a picturesque group of adventurers, parvenus, tradesmen, professional poets, fortune hunters, and petty provincial magistrates. It is an interesting fact that in this novel of Petronius women for the first time, in so far as I know, play an important part in literature. The narrative literature of the earlier period deals mainly with the doings of men and their relations to one another, and it is primarily addressed to men. A late writer has acutely surmised that the romance of chivalry was written for women, and that we owe to them the beginnings of the modern novel. What has just been noted of the Satiræ of Petronius would indicate the same origin for the ancient novel with equal probability.

In Greek and Roman epic and tragic poetry a primary motive was regularly employed which is not regarded as essential in modern literature; I mean the wrath of an offended deity or the unpitying action of fate. It is true that heredity in the prose dramas of Ibsen and society in many of the so-called problem novels of to-day serve the same dramatic purpose, but that element is not an *essential* one with us, and a modern author in composing a piece of imaginative literature would not feel bound to introduce it. We are likely, therefore, to forget that it *was* an essential factor with the Romans. Although he was creating a new form of literature, Petronius observes literary conventions in introducing this factor. The mishaps of his rascally hero are due to the anger of Priapus, who was as much an object of ridicule as of reverence among the Romans. The introduction of this motive and the choice of this god as the offended deity give a unity to the story, and make it a delightful satire upon the epic. The hero, Encolpius, driven by his rascalities from one town to another, becomes a realistic Odysseus. The book satisfies our modern conception of a novel, then, in having a well-defined plot, and it may also truly be said of it, I think, that each incident is a natural result of the action of two forces, the character of the hero and his environment. It must be confessed, however, that the development of the plot is not followed out as continuously in this ancient novel as it is in a modern one. Long episodes are introduced which do not help along the action, and the movement is frequently interrupted by literary disquisitions or by poems.

In one important particular the novel of Petronius stands apart from all ancient imaginative literature and takes its place by the side of our latest modern fiction: I mean in its realism. This is true of its individual incidents, of its portrayal of contemporaneous society, and of the way in which the various characters are presented. I have already mentioned the skill of Petronius in reproducing local color. But since the treatment is intensely realistic, while we have a true picture of a certain class, the romance of Petronius gives us a one-sided view of contemporaneous society, just as realistic novels of the same type do to-day. The realistic treatment which Petronius has adopted in his novel puts it in marked contrast to the early Greek romances, which appeared somewhat later. The Marvellous Things Beyond Thule is a fair specimen of these productions. The hero and the heroine in this story, Dinias and Dercyllis by name, after surviving perils at the hands of robbers, assassins, and magicians; after witnessing murders, suicides, and resurrections; having exhausted the possibilities of adventure from Hades to the North Pole — are finally transported to the moon to round off their experiences.

I am not aware that any one has called attention to the fact that the modern realistic novel made its first appearance in circumstances very similar to those in which the romance of Petronius was written. It is equally remarkable that in both cases the same phase of society is represented. The state of society in Spain in the sixteenth century, when the picaresque novel appeared, was the same as that of Italy in the first century of our era. In both countries the old aristocracy had disappeared, and a plutocracy had taken its place. The importation of slave labor had driven the peasant proprietors out of the country districts of Italy, while in Spain a similar result was produced by the heavy taxes which made agriculture unprofitable. The Inquisition in Spain, like the *delatio* in Italy, developed a spirit of suspicion and selfishness, and broke the ties which ordinarily bind men to one another. The ancient and the modern realistic novel grew in similar soils. The resemblance which the Spanish novel bears to its Latin predecessor is still more striking. Both are rogue stories; both are autobiographical; both are based on a careful study of society. Magic, the supernatural, and the element of perilous adventure are carefully excluded. The Spaniard as well as the Italian has made free use of the folk tale. His work, like that of Petronius, has a marked element of satire in it; and it bears the same relation to the romance of chivalry that the Latin novel bears to the epic. Such a marked resemblance in treatment would on *a priori* grounds lead one to think that Mendoza and Aleman found their inspiration in the Satiræ of Petronius, but there seems to be no reason for supposing that either of them was familiar with the work of the Roman. The Italian and the Spanish realistic novel were spontaneous products of a similar situation.

One of the fundamental principles of modern realism, as enunciated, for instance, by Zola and Howells and Garland, is that the characters of the persons concerned shall be revealed to the reader by their words and actions, without comment or explanation on the part of the author. This principle has been scrupulously observed by Petronius, and there is not a single instance in his novel where the artist destroys the illusion by obtruding his own personality into the scene he is painting. As for his characters, they stand out with marvellous distinctness — the roué Encolpius, the poetaster Eumolpus, the parvenu Trimalchio, and the shrewd housewife Fortunata. Even the minor characters are portrayed with as much clearness and individuality as the figures in one of Meissonier's pictures. Let me try to convey a feeble impression from Petronius's own book of his cleverness in portraying minor characters and of the humor and sprightliness of his dialogue. The scene is a dinner party given by a parvenu. The guests are all or almost all freedmen, a rag merchant, a retired dealer in tombstones, an after-dinner poet, and men of that type. Conversation has become general under the mellowing influence of the Falernian, and the tedious, tactless Seleucus, who has just come from a funeral, discourses in a maudlin fashion on the insignificance of man in the economy of nature, and proceeds to describe in detail the last sickness of his friend and the scenes at his funeral, until the plain speaker Phileros cuts short his lugubrious tale by remarking that the dear departed would pull a copper out of the mud with his teeth, if he got a chance, and that, having lived seventy years and left a round hundred thousand, he ought to have been satisfied. Ganymedes, the pessimist of the company, has been waiting impatiently for Phileros to bring his remarks to an end, and with that delightful inconsequence which characterizes the conversation of men of his type begins a long lament for the good old times, when the worthy Safinius flourished, whose oratorical power depended not on the new-fangled arts of logic and composition, but on the strength of his voice. With the men of that time you could play *mora* in the dark, but as for our days — well, the less said the better, and in view of the prevalent dishonesty and irreligion it's no wonder that times are bad and that the gods are rheumatic when we ask them to come to our relief. But the rag dealer,

Echion, has no such gloomy views of the Fatherland. It's all in the way you look at things. In fact, if you lived somewhere else, you would be saying that pigs walked the streets here already roasted. In reality the future is very bright, for Titus is going to give a show at the amphitheatre, and there's every prospect of a fight to the finish, and it won't be anything like the show which Glyce gave with his hamstrung gladiators, who were ready to drop if you blew at them. And so the dinner goes merrily on, until the host, whose vanity grows more evident, calls for his will to be read. The reading of the will draws forth such loud wails and cries of lamentation from the slaves, who have an eye single to their own advancement, that the local fire company supposes the host's house to be on fire and comes rushing in with axes and ladders. The dinner is brought to an inglorious end. All of this — and the whole story, in fact — is told with delightful cynicism, a sparkling wit, and with charming simplicity and lucidity of style.

Quintilian, the great Roman literary critic, confessed by implication that satire was the only new form of literature which his countrymen had produced, and critics of subsequent times have in the main accepted his *dictum*. It seems to me, however, that the Romans may successfully lay claim to the creation of prose fiction also. There is no earlier extant novel than that of Petronius, nor is there any reference in ancient literature to an earlier work of that sort, so far as I know, so that Petronius is at the same time the creator of a new *genre* of literature and the author of one of the world's greatest pieces of realistic fiction.

A ROMAN PURITAN

ONE ventures with some diffidence upon the task of discussing the work of an author like the Roman poet Persius, whose writings are not widely known and are not highly esteemed by many who know them. But the obscurity in which Persius languishes is, it seems to me, undeserved; for his poetry has an intrinsic value; he speaks for a class of men who have made a deep impression upon history; and any knowledge which we may gain of the influences at work in the first century of our era, in which his lot was cast, will doubtless always be of special value in our eyes.

But whatever may be the attitude of the world in general toward Persius, to the New Englander he should be a writer of peculiar interest. Perhaps he of all men can most thoroughly understand his temperament and ideals; for an intimate acquaintance with the characteristics of the New England Puritan can best give one a correct view of the attitude of the Roman poet toward men and things; while a knowledge of the circumstances under which Puritanism developed will enable one to understand the times in which Persius lived and the motives and practices which he attacked, since the moral and intellectual condition of Rome under the Cæsars was not essentially unlike that of England under the Stuarts. The spirit of the times was distinctly one of materialism and formalism. Rome and Italy were at the beginning of the Christian era secure from invasion; peace brought in its train a desire for ease and luxury; the provinces sent their rich tribute to Rome to satisfy this desire, while the attractions of the metropolis, the introduction of slave labor everywhere throughout Italy, and the consequent displacement of free labor, brought an immense idle population to the city, whose eager demands for bread and the games brooked no refusal. Matthew Arnold has divided the English people of to-day into barbarians, philistines and populace. In the Rome of Persius, the philistines, that great middle class which preserves longest the homely virtues as well as the narrow prejudices of a people, had in large measure disappeared. There were left a vulgarized aristocracy and a brutalized proletariat. By the side of this materialism was a formalism in the higher activities of life like that against which the English Puritan inveighed. Sacrifices were still made in the temples, the people still met as if to choose their magistrates, but effective faith in the old Roman gods was dead and the political assemblies of the people only registered the wishes of the emperor.

It was in a society of this sort, a society whose vices and weaknesses Juvenal scourges and Martial complacently paints, that Persius passed his life. In his own writings Persius, unlike Horace, his predecessor in satire, tells us little about himself, but a brief memoir from an unknown hand gives us the essential facts of his life. He was born in 34 A. D., in a little town of Etruria, and died in 62. His family was one of rank and wealth, and he was able to secure the training in literature and philosophy which his studious tastes craved. He had a pleasing appearance, was gentle in his manner, modest and abstemious. The large property which he left behind him at death he bequeathed to his mother and sister, while his library, which, significantly enough, was made up of the seven hundred volumes of the philosopher Chrysippus, was left to his Stoic teacher, Cornutus. One of the most charming passages in his satires, one of the few passages, in fact, in which he unbends, is that in which he expresses his gratitude to his friend and teacher: "When the purple garb of youth resigned its dreaded guardianship, and the toys of my boyhood were cast aside and hung up as an offering to the quaint old household gods, when my comrades enticed me and the snow-white toga of manhood proclaimed my right to cast my eyes at will over the whole Subura, I threw myself as a son into thine arms, and thou didst take me up, Cornutus, in my tender years into thy Socratic bosom."

The friendship and counsel of Cornutus and of his other Stoic teachers was indeed the determining factor in his early life. This group of Stoics to which Persius attached himself was made of the same stern stuff as our Puritan ancestors under Cromwell; and many of them, like Pætus Thrasea, their leader, suffered martyrdom rather than abate one jot or tittle of their ethical or political creed. They accepted Cato of Utica as their model, and had no sympathy with the school of Seneca, that great teacher of their time, who sought to adapt the principles of Stoic philosophy to the practices of the Roman court. The sympathies of Persius lay with this faction of the Stoic school, for, as his biographer tells us, he knew Seneca, but was not attracted by him, and it is interesting to note that one of his earliest compositions consisted of verses in commemoration of his kinswoman Arria, of whose tragic death Pliny tells us. The story is a favorite one with Latin writers. Arria's husband, Pætus, was charged with participation in a conspiracy against the Emperor Claudius — unjustly, and yet his conviction was sure. Without waiting for the outcome of the trial, Arria in the presence of her husband drew a dagger, plunged it into her breast, and after drawing it out, handed it to her husband, saying, "It does not hurt, Pætus." The fact that he was brought up under such influences and drew his inspiration from such incidents as these gave to Persius, who was an idealist, whose only knowledge of the world was that which may be had from one's study windows, that intensity of purpose which characterizes his poetry, his narrow and distorted view of men and things, and even that tone of cant of which we seem to catch an echo now and then in his verses.

From his absorbing faith in Stoicism and his desire to rescue those who did not know its teachings from their ignorance and vice came his impulse to write. His inspiration springs from the same overmastering desire as does that of Lucretius; and it is a noteworthy fact that the most impressive expositions which we have in Latin of the tenets of Epicureanism and Stoicism, the two most influential schools of philosophy in Rome, are in verse, in the poems of Lucretius and Persius. It is not strange that Persius should have chosen satire as the literary vehicle of his thoughts. Greek philosophy in passing through the transforming alembic of the Roman mind acquired a practical character and was developed on the side of ethics. Stoicism in Rome taught, as one has said, "purer conceptions of God, broader views of humanity, the supremacy of the will over the passions, of eternal duty over temporal expediency." Now, the recognized literary medium for the correction of vice and instruction in virtue is satire. It was a natural thing for Persius, therefore, to adopt this form of composition. His own uncompromising attitude also toward the vices and weaknesses of mankind made the choice a natural one. Perhaps, too, a perusal of the works of his great predecessor, Lucilius, may have influenced his decision, as his biographer intimates.

But the doctrines which Persius wishes to teach are of such transcendent importance that literature, at the best, is an unsatisfactory means by which to accomplish his purpose. He does not hesitate, therefore, to express his contempt for literary art and for literature itself. It is but the chattering of parrots, and finds its inspiration in the need of bread and butter. "Who made the parrot so glib with his 'Good morning,' and who taught the magpie to attempt the feat of talking like men? That great teacher of art and giver of mother wit, the stomach." Of his own inspiration he is equally contemptuous. "I have not bathed my lips in the spring of the hack, nor do I remember to have dreamed on two-peaked Parnassus, so as to burst upon the stage as a full-fledged poet. It is but as a poor half-brother of the guild that I bring my verses to the festival of the worshipful poets' company."

In view of his attitude toward literature, his disregard of literary usage in the construction of the satire does not surprise us. Following his predecessor, Horace, he adopts the dialogue form at the beginning of his satires, but like a disputant who is convinced of the truth of his own cause and the weakness of his adversary's logic, he brooks no opposition, and the second speaker is soon overwhelmed and disappears under the torrent of the poet's invective. We shall find later another factor also, which contributed to the same result.

In one of his Lowell lectures Prince Wolkonsky has brought out in a luminous way the dual personality of his countryman, Tolstoi, the artist, and philosopher. He has shown that the two are at variance with each other in Tolstoi's writings, and that at one moment it is the philosopher who speaks, at another the artist. The same statement may be made with truth of our Roman writer. The Stoic Persius finds literature and literary art vanity and vexation of spirit; but the poet Persius escapes at times from the domination of his other self and gives us a touch of real life or a bit of imaginative writing. Now and then the philosopher, or rather the moralist, and the poet are in harmony. Such is the case when he concludes his impassioned arraignment of the materialism and formalism which characterized the religion of his day. "Let us rather give to the gods of heaven such an offering as the degenerate son of the great Messalla has no means of giving even out of his huge sacrificial charger, — a soul in which duty to God and man are rightly blended, purity in the inmost recesses of the heart, a breast filled with the sense of honor and nobility. Let me have these to carry to the temple, and a handful of meal shall win me acceptance."

Inspired as Persius was by a singleness of purpose to teach the truth of Stoicism, it is not strange that almost all of his satires are based upon some dogma of the Stoic creed. One is an attack upon shams, another an invective against low spiritual standards, while in a third the thesis is established that all save the wise men are slaves. To state the doctrines which our poet teaches in his satires would be equivalent to summarizing the creed of Puritanism. The dogma that all men are slaves is but the ancient version of total depravity. The saving remnant of the wise men are the elect of the New England Puritan. The doctrine that we are what God has willed us to be might have been taken from the popular Calvinistic creed of our New England fathers; and when Persius teaches that he who offends in one point offends in all, he is only anticipating the Mosaic dogma of the Massachusetts and Connecticut minister, while pervading all is that intensity of conviction and that practical belief in the transcendent importance of questions of theology and morals which cast so sombre a hue over the whole life of our New England ancestors. In fact, when I read the verses of Persius I seem to be sitting where I sat as a boy, in a high-backed pew of the old meeting-house, listening to the minister as he expounds the doctrines of foreordination, of election, and original sin.

The view which we have taken of Persius throws light upon that much-vexed question of his relation to Horace. Horace adopts the dialogue form in his satires, and preserves the identity of his characters with great circumspection, and his characters are men of flesh and blood. Persius attempts to follow his predecessor in this particular, but his speakers soon fade away into the indefinite "you." This difference in literary method illustrates well the essential difference in character between the two men. Horace's conclusions are based upon his own observation of individuals. His words are therefore addressed to individuals and his arguments are based upon practical truths adapted to each particular case. Persius is so overwhelmed by the truth of his proposition and its applicability to all men, that he is not content with assailing all through one, but he must reach the whole world directly. Furthermore Cicero, with his tolerant eclecticism, and Horace, with his comfortable epicureanism, recognized the good as well as the bad in human nature. Both of them, trained in the school of experience, had come to look with a forgiving eye upon the foibles and weaknesses of mankind. But in the Puritanical philosophy of the young idealist, Persius, he who breaks the law in one point breaks it in all, and there is no line of difference to be drawn between the great sin and the little sin. The Socratic dialogue, therefore, which assumes that the second speaker has at least some show of reason on his side, and which both Cicero and Horace adopt in their discussions of manners and morals, is quite unsuitable for one who believes that his opponent is radically wrong and utterly illogical. Persius is true, then, to his philosophical conviction in neglecting the dialogue form of composition.

But Persius admires Horace. He follows him in fact as a literary model, and borrows turns of expression and illustrations from him constantly. The result is that, while the characters in Horace are drawn from life and stand out distinctly in the foreground, those in Persius are only reflections from the canvas of his predecessor. It is easy to find the reason for this difference in the different training which the two men received. Horace's philosophy is a practical one. His conclusions have been reached from an inductive study of the facts coming under his own observation. The order with Persius is the reverse: First the principle, then its application to real life. The individual is therefore only an evanescent illustration, one of a thousand. The dropping of a stone from the roof of a house illustrates the operation of the law of gravity; but we do not wait with suspended judgment to see whether it will fall or not, for the existence of the law should be already known to every thinking creature. With such a contempt, therefore, for the individual case, it was quite natural for Persius, when casting about him for an illustration, to take it not from contemporary society, but from the pages of Horace, which he had before him, without due regard sometimes to the appropriateness of the example.

Yet, strange to say, Persius is not lacking in dramatic power. These, for instance, are the words in which he describes the real punishment for sin and the true terrors of remorse: "We pray thee, O Father of the Gods, to punish the monsters of tyranny in no other wise than this, — let them look upon virtue and grieve that they have lost her forever. Were the groans from the brazen bull of Sicily more terrible or did the sword that hung from the gilded cornice strike more dread into the princely neck beneath it than that state of mind when a man whispers to himself, 'I am going headlong to ruin,' and palcs, unhappy wretch, at a thought which the very wife of his bosom may not share?"

Persius is, in fact, terribly in earnest. He is not the mere philosopher who expounds abstract principles, without caring whether they are applied or not. He is also a moralist, and a moralist of the school to which John Knox, John Wesley, and Whitefield belonged, a moralist who sees the impassable chasm which lies between good and evil and who believes in the natural depravity of all men and the moral death which threatens them. Such men have always been endowed with great dramatic power, and Persius is no exception to the rule. Indeed it is in the possession of this quality that his chief merit as a poet consists.

PETRARCH'S LETTERS TO CICERO

GEORG VOIGT in his Wiederbelebung des klassischen Alterthums speaks of Petrarch as *der Entdecker der neuen Welt des Humanismus*, and, in view of the part which he played in the Revival of Learning, these words of praise are not extravagant. In the catalogues which have come down to us from the Middle Ages one finds now and then the title of a Greek or Latin classic, and a few men of learning would seem to have taken some interest in reading these books; but long before Petrarch's day real knowledge of the works of antiquity was at a low ebb. Even Dante came but little under the influence of the new learning.

With Petrarch the new era begins. His energy and care in collecting and preserving those works of the past which were already known, his enthusiasm in bringing to light books which had fallen into oblivion, his sympathy with the classical spirit, and his power to inspire others gave the first impulse to the new movement and were potent factors in advancing it.

His interest in Latin literature dated back to his boyhood days, and is well illustrated by a story of his early life. Petrarch's father, who was an advocate, intended to have his son take up the profession of law, and with this object in view sent him to Bologna, but after a time, feeling that the young man was not advancing as rapidly as he expected, the father sought for the reason of his son's slow progress, and found it in the shape of a large collection of the Latin classics concealed under Petrarch's bed. These were thrown unceremoniously into the fire, but the grief and anger which Petrarch showed induced his father to save a Cicero and a Virgil from the flames, and revealed the depth of the young man's passion for Latin literature. This passion animated him through life, for in later years, he tells us in one of his letters, whenever on making a journey he noticed a monastery near the road, he invariably turned aside to see if he could discover a book not in his own collection. Not content with his own investigations he sent requests and urgent entreaties to friends and acquaintances in Italy, France, Germany, and England for any books which could be found in the neighborhood of his correspondents. The works of Cicero were the special objects of his search, and by his indefatigable efforts he brought to light, among other things, the Philippics of that author, some of his philosophical works, and the orations for Archias and for Milo.

The crowning event of Petrarch's life, however, lay in the discovery of a collection of Cicero's Letters in the cathedral library at Verona in 1345 A. D., and, although he was weary and ill at the time, he would not intrust the manuscript to other hands, but he himself made a copy of it. He regarded the book as his most precious possession, and so highly did he prize it that he never allowed a copy to be made of it, but he published the knowledge of his discovery to the world in a letter addressed to Cicero himself. This letter possesses a double interest for us. It was written when Petrarch was full of the first joy of his discovery, and therefore fixes the date and the place at which Cicero's Letters were made known to the world again. It records also the first impressions which Petrarch received from reading the familiar letters which Cicero wrote to his intimate friends. He had read some of the orations and some of the philosophical works of Cicero. Now he took up the letters for the first time, and it is interesting to compare Petrarch's impressions with those which we form to-day, for we also usually read the writings of Cicero in the same order. His letter runs as follows:

FRANCIS PETRARCH SENDS GREETINGS TO M. TULLIUS CICERO

Thy letters, sought long and earnestly, and found where I least thought to find them, I have read with the greatest eagerness. I have listened to thee, Marcus Tullius, as thou didst talk of many matters, as thou didst lament many ills, as thou didst throw upon many subjects the transforming light of thine intelligence, and I, who had long known what sort of a guide thou hadst been to others, have at last understood what kind of a man thou wert to thyself. Do thou in turn, wherever thou art, listen to this one word, which is inspired by true love for thee, a word not now of advice but of regret, to which one of the after world who is most devoted to thy memory has given utterance not without tears. Thou who wert ever restless and full of anxiety, or that thou mayest hear again thine own words, O headstrong and unfortunate old man, why hast thou plunged into so many struggles and quarrels which would profit thee in no wise whatsoever? Where hast thou left the peace of mind which befitted both thine age and thy profession and thy fortune? What counterfeit glitter of fame has involved thee as an old man in wars where young men fought, and hurried thee, the sport of every blast of fortune, to a death unworthy of a philosopher? Alas! unmindful both of a brother's advice and of thine own wholesome precepts — many as they are — like a traveller by night waving a torch in the darkness, thou hast shown to those who should follow the path upon which thou thyself hast so sadly slipped. I say nothing of Dionysius, I say nothing of thy brother and nephew, I say nothing, if thou dost not wish it, even of Dolabella himself, all of whom thou art now exalting to heaven with words of praise, and now abusing with unexpected maledictions. Perchance these acts of thine could be overlooked. I pass over Julius Cæsar also, whose well-tried clemency became a haven of refuge for those who attacked him. Furthermore, I say nothing of Pompeius Magnus, with whom, through a certain tie of intimacy, thou didst seem to have power without limit. But what madness incited thee against Antony? It was love of the Republic, I suppose, the Republic which thou didst confess was already utterly ruined. But if it was true loyalty, if it was love of liberty which led thee on, a view which one may hold in the case of so great a man, why so close an intimacy with Augustus? What reply wilt thou make, pray, to thy friend Brutus? If it be true, he says,[1] that Octavius pleases thee, thou wilt not seem to have avoided a master, but to have sought a more friendly master. This unhappy event was reserved for thee, and this was the crowning misfortune in thy career, Cicero, that of this very man whom thou hadst praised so highly thou shouldst speak bitterly, I will not say because he did thee harm, but because he did not withstand those who were doing thee harm. I grieve at thy lot, my friend, I feel shame and pity at the thought of thy great mistakes; and now like this very Brutus I give no credit to those precepts, in which I know thou wert thoroughly versed. What profits it forsooth to teach others; what boots it to speak always of the virtues in the most fitting language, if meanwhile thou dost not listen to thyself? Ah! how much better it would have been for a philosopher, of all men, to have grown old in the country far from strife, while thinking, as thou dost thyself say in one place, of the life everlasting, and not of this present brief existence; how much better not to have had the *fasces*, not to have eagerly craved a triumph, how much better had a Catiline never excited thine anger. But of this we talk in vain. Farewell forever, my Cicero. In the world above, on the right bank

[1] In an extant letter to Cicero (*ad Brut.* I, 16, 1) which is probably spurious, however.

of the Athesis, in the city of Verona in Transpadane Italy, on the sixteenth day before the Kalends of the fifth month, in the year from the birth of that Christ whom thou didst not know, thirteen hundred and forty-five.

The first perusal of Cicero's Letters proved a shock to Petrarch. Could this vain and vacillating mortal, who taught men to be strong and temperate, while he himself was weak and passionate, be the Cicero who had thundered against a Catiline and an Antony, whose praise of philosophy had charmed even St. Augustine? But as Petrarch read the letters again a new light broke upon him. The words of confidence which one pours into the ear of his "other self" should not condemn a man any more than the questionings of one's own heart. If Cicero's broad view of the future made him hesitate when a narrow-minded man saw only the straight path of duty before him, yet in the end he followed duty, and his genius at last was still a source of inspiration and life, and the recognition of this last fact inspired Petrarch to the composition of another letter to Cicero six months after the one already given.

FRANCIS PETRARCH SENDS GREETING TO M. TULLIUS CICERO

If my former letter offended thee, for what thy friend in the Andria says, as thou thyself art wont to remark, is true, that "complaisance maketh friends, truth begetteth hatred," listen to that which may in part appease the anger of thy soul, and let not truth always be hateful in thine eyes, for we are angry at true words of blame, we are pleased by true words of praise. It is true, Cicero, and let me say it with thy consent, that thou didst live as a man, thou didst speak as an orator, thou didst write as a philosopher. It was thy life with which I found fault, not thy talent nor thine eloquence; in fact, I wonder at the one, I am lost in admiration of the other. And yet in thy life I find nothing lacking save steadfastness and the love of repose, which belongs of right to a philosopher's life, and a desire to avoid civil wars — since freedom was dead and the Republic already buried amid the sorrows of its adherents.

See in what a different way I treat thee from the way in which thou didst treat Epicurus in many places, but in particular in the work, De Finibus.[1] For thou dost everywhere approve of his life, while thou dost ridicule his claims to talent. I ridicule thee in no wise, still, as I have said, I feel a compassion for thee

[1] For instance, *De Fin.* II, 80.

in view of thy life, I congratulate thee upon thy genius and thine eloquence. O most exalted father of Roman eloquence, not I alone, but all of us who are adorned with the beauties of the Latin tongue, render thee our thanks; for we refresh our fields from thy streams, we frankly confess that we have been directed by thy guidance, aided by thine opinions, and illumined by thy light; that finally under thine auspices, so to say, we have gained this power and inspiration to write, however small it may be. Another has come into our lives also, as a guide upon the path of poetry; since necessity called for one whom we might follow as he advanced with the free step of the poet, a leader, too (in prose) of measured tread it sought, one whose speech, one whose songs, we might admire, since if both of you will pardon me, neither was a master in both prose and poetry. He is no match for thee in breadth of vision nor thou for him in the perception of subtleties. Perchance I am not the first to say this, however deeply I feel it; in fact one expressed this opinion before I did, or rather he said the sentiment had been expressed by others — a great man, too, Annæus Seneca,[1] of Cordova, from whom, as this very man complains, not thine old age indeed, but the fury of the civil wars took thee. He *could* have seen thee, but he *did* not see thee; still he was an enthusiastic eulogist of thy works

[1] Seneca, the rhetorician, was born in 54 B. C., *i. e.*, eleven years before Cicero's death.

and of the works of the other writer referred to above. In his pages, therefore, each person circumscribed by his own limitations in the way of eloquence is bidden to yield to thee, his contemporary, and to take his place among the many. But I torment thee with curiosity; who, pray, is this leader, thou dost ask? Thou knowest the man, if only thou dost remember his name. It is Publius Virgilius Maro, a citizen of Mantua, of whom thou didst prophesy illustrious things. For when, as we read in the books, after admiring a certain juvenile little work of his, thou hadst inquired who the author was, and hadst thyself, already an old man, seen him, who was a youth, thou wert delighted, and from the inexhaustible fountain of thine eloquence, thou didst render him a tribute, combined, it is true, with praise of thyself, yet well-founded and glorious and honorable. For thou didst say, "Rome's second great hope." And this saying, heard from thy lips, pleased him in such a degree, and remained so firmly in his memory, that twenty years afterward, when thou hadst been long removed from the affairs of men, he placed it in his divine work in exactly the same words, and had it been permitted thee to see this work, thou wouldst have rejoiced to think that from the first flower thou hadst foreseen so unerringly the fruit destined to come. Likewise thou wouldst have congratulated the Latin Muses because they had either left a doubtful victory to the haughty Greeks, or wrested a sure one from them; for each opinion has its sponsors. I doubt not that thou, if from thy books I have learned thy mind, which I seem to myself to know as if I had lived with thee, I doubt not that thou, I say, wilt be the champion of the latter view, and that as thou hast given to Latium the palm in oratory,[1] so thou wilt in poetry, and that thou wilt have already bidden the Iliad to yield to the Æneid, which concession from the very beginning of Virgil's work Propertius did not hesitate to demand. For when he contemplated the beginnings of the Pierian work, what he thought of them and what he hoped, he proclaimed openly in these verses:

> "I cry you, yield ye Roman writers, yield ye Greeks;
> An offspring greater than the Iliad is born?"[2]

So much for the second Latin leader in eloquence and the second hope of mighty Rome; now I return to thee. What I think of thy life, what of thy genius thou hast heard. Thou art waiting to hear of thy books, what fortune has befallen them, to what extent they are admired, whether it be by the common people or by the learned. There are extant then noble works of thine which we are able, let me not say, to read through, nay, not even to enumerate. The fame of thy deeds is widespread, and thy name is great and fills the ears of men; but the studious are very few in number, whether

[1] *Tusc. Disp.* I, 3.

[2] Prop. III, 26, 65–6.

the cause lie in the sternness of the times or in the dulness and sluggishness of men's minds, or what I the rather think, in the greed for gain which drives the thoughts of men toward other ends. Therefore some of thy books, unless I am deceived, have without doubt been lost, perhaps hopelessly, to us who live to-day; to my great grief, to the great shame of our generation, to the great loss of posterity. For it has not seemed shameful enough to neglect the cultivation of our own talents, so that coming generations receive therefrom nothing of profit, but we must needs bring to naught the fruit of thy labor and of the labor of thy countrymen by a neglect utterly cruel and intolerable. For what I lament has happened in the case of thy books and in the case of many works of illustrious men. As my remarks just now were concerning thy books, these are the titles of those whose loss is the more noteworthy: the De Re Publica, the De Re Familiari, the De Re Militari, the De Laude Philosophiae, the De Consolatione, and the De Gloria, although with reference to this last work, there is rather an uncertain hope than a fixed despair.[1] Nay, we have lost large parts even of thine extant works, so that, just as if they had been overwhelmed in a great struggle by oblivion and neglect, we must mourn for leaders, some of

[1] A manuscript which he believed to be one of the De Gloria Petrarch had loaned to a friend. It was not returned, and no manuscript of the work has been found since that time.

whom are dead, others, mutilated or lost. For this state of things, which we suffer in the case of many other books, exists especially with reference to the Academica and the books upon the Orator and the Laws, which have survived in so mutilated and disfigured a condition that it would really have been better for them had they perished.

Now thou dost wish to hear of the condition of the city of Rome and of the Roman State, to learn what the state of the fatherland is, to know in what degree the citizens are harmonious, to whom the control of affairs has fallen, by what hands the reins of government are held — whether wisely managed or not; whether the Danube and the Ganges, the Ebro and the Nile and the Don are our boundary lines; or has some leader risen "to limit our sway by the ocean, our fame by the stars,"[1] or "to extend our domain beyond the Garamantes and the Indians,"[2] as says that Mantuan friend of thine. I surmise that thou wilt hear most eagerly these things and things like them; for thy loyalty increases this natural eagerness, and thy love for the fatherland, leading even to thy ruin, is known to every one. But it may be better to say nothing. For believe me, Cicero, if thou shalt have heard in what condition our affairs are, tears will fall from thine eyes in whatever portion of the world above or the world below

[1] Virg. *Aen.* I, 287.
[2] *Ibid.* VI, 794.

thou dost chance to be. Farewell forever. In the world above, upon the left bank of the Rhone in Transalpine Gaul in the same year, on the 16th day before the Kalends of January.

LITERATURE AND THE COMMON PEOPLE OF ROME

IN the last twenty-five years or more the study of political history has undergone a marked change. The common people, as the true subject-matter of the historian's study, have come into their rights. We hear more of their political aspirations and social conditions, less of the policies and ambitious plans of their rulers and leaders. Can we apply this new method of studying the Roman people to the field of literature as well as to that of politics? We have made our estimates of the great Roman writers and have fixed the place which their productions are to hold in the world's literary history. Can we turn now to the average Roman and get any light on his literary interests and his appreciation of literature? We shall find no categorical statements to help us from contemporary sources, because the professional writer, like Arbuscula, the actress, probably had a profound contempt for the judgment of the common people in such matters; but a bit of evidence here and a bit there will assist us in answering the question, and lead us to a truer estimate of this side of Roman civilization, I hope. How the Greeks would be rated, if such a study were made of them no one of us would doubt. The intellectual acuteness and the high æsthetic standards of the average citizen of Athens are rarely called in question. Even those whose sympathies lie with the aims and tendencies of modern society freely recognize these qualities in Greek civilization.

The common people of Rome never reached the high plane which the Athenians attained in this respect, and they have suffered, suffered unduly, I think, in comparison with their more cultured neighbors. We often seem to me in our study of historical people and events to show too great a pleasure in contrasts. If with Mommsen, for instance, we brand Cicero as a political time-server, the far-sightedness of his great contemporary Cæsar will stand out the more clearly. If, on the other hand, we take a more favorable view of Cicero's character, we are prone to touch up the dark spots in his career, to paint him as the champion of law and order, with the sombre figure of Cæsar, the revolutionist, by his side, to make the contrast. We are inclined to follow the same practice in our treatment of two peoples who show certain points of difference. By exaggerating these and by obscuring their points of similarity we stimulate the imagination, secure for the reader a clear mental picture of the two contrasted peoples, and heighten the dramatic effect. It is convenient, too, to label and pigeon-hole people and things. It is simple and has a show of system to say that the Greeks had æsthetic qualities but no political steadiness; that the Romans showed marvellous political genius, but lacked an appreciation of the finer things of life. Our estimate of the Romans in this matter has suffered from both these tendencies, to contrast and to classify. So far as our judgment of them is concerned, it was unfortunate that fate did not put Rome a thousand years earlier or later and thus save us from the temptation of using such light and dark colors respectively in drawing our outlines of the two peoples. It was this unkindness of fate, I fancy, which is partly responsible for the common belief that the Romans were philistines in art and literature, for the feeling for instance, that Mummius, the conqueror of Corinth, was a typical Roman. The story connected with his name will be recalled We are told that when he was bringing back from Corinth the priceless works of art which he had taken in the capture of the city, he stipulated with the owners of the vessels who transported them that if they were lost at sea "they should be replaced by others of equal value."

This natural tendency to set up a comparison between the Greeks and the Romans has colored our estimates of the Romans in another way, it seems to me. Most of us will freely confess, I presume, that their literary productions fall below those of the Greeks in originality and in perfection of form. But do we stop to think that in passing this judgment we are estimating the achievements of their professional literary men? They were undoubtedly under the domination of the Greeks. It could not have been otherwise. In the third century before Christ, at the very beginning of Rome's literary history, her writers were brought into contact with the highly perfected literature of Greece. If they had not striven to imitate it they would have sinned against the light, and yet when I speculate on what they might have done in the field of literature if their national genius had been allowed to follow its natural lines of development, I sometimes find my sympathy going out to the elder Cato in his fierce Chauvinistic protest against everything of Greek origin. The Romans, like their Trojan ancestors, might well have feared the Greeks even when they were bringing gifts. Let us frankly confess that professional writers among the Romans never escaped entirely from the influence of their great models, but let us not extend our judgment to the common people and tacitly assume that they were lacking in the æsthetic sense because that faculty, from lack of opportunity, never showed any signs of independent development among the professional literary men and artists of Rome.

It is important to distinguish between these two elements in the population in asking ourselves who the favorite authors of the Romans were. In making their choice of Greek plays for adaptation into Latin Plautus and Terence have indicated their preferences clearly enough. Cicero's frequent quotations from Ennius reveal his great admiration for that author and his intimate acquaintance with his writings. Horace tells us his likes and dislikes in almost every one of his literary Satires and Epistles, and in one of them we see him setting out for the country with copies of Plato, Menander, Eupolis, and Archilochus packed up in his luggage. But who were the favorite poets of the people? With what Latin writers were they familiar? What kind of literature did they admire? What were their literary standards?

Perhaps among any people the condition of the drama furnishes the safest and clearest indication of literary taste. In an age when the circulation of literature in a written form was inconsiderable it is our only means of judgment. If we apply this test to the Roman people, and turn first to Plautus and Terence, we naturally call to mind the apologetic tone which Terence takes in several of his prologues, which seems to imply a slight interest in the drama on the part of his contemporaries; yet a careful reading of these prologues brings out clearly the fact that Terence was not disturbed about the attitude of the great body of his audience, but was defending himself against the strictures on his technique of the new dramatic school, led by the rival poet Luscius Lanuvinus. In fact, the Eunuchus won such immediate approval at the hands of the people that, if we may believe Suetonius, it was brought out twice in the same day. However, the well-known prologues of the Hecyra have been thought to show conclusively the absence of real literary interest on the part of the Romans. Twice the play had been attempted, and both times it had failed to hold the audience. On its first presentation, as the veteran actor Ambivius states in his pathetic appeal for a hearing, a company of rope dancers outside emptied the theatre; at the second trial the rumor that a gladiatorial performance was going on raised such an uproar that the actors were unable to proceed. When I read the Hecyra I am almost inclined to think that the unfavorable reception with which it met indicates rather good literary judgment on the part of the Roman audience than an absence of literary taste. It is confessedly the weakest of Terence's plays, and the early part in particular is tedious. Then too, in trying to draw a correct inference from an incident like this one, ought we not to bear in mind the difference between the Anglo-Saxon and the Southern temperaments? We are chary with our applause and our expressions of disapproval. Southern audiences are to-day, and were in Terence's time, as unrestrained in their outbursts of disapproval as they are quick in expressing their admiration of a play. The popularity of Plautus admits of no question. It could be shown from the confident tone of his prologues if it were not attested by the vogue which his plays had long after his death. A still more convincing proof that the comedies of Plautus and his successors appealed to the popular taste lies in the fact that the Roman officials, in arranging the great national festivals in the spring, summer, and autumn, regularly included dramatic performances in their programme. Now, as we know, there was a close connection between politics and the drama, for most of the Roman festivals were under the direction of ambitious young officials whose political future depended largely on their success in giving entertainments which pleased the people. Both the modern and the ancient theatrical manager must draw full houses — one to make money, the other to win votes. If the plays of Plautus and Terence had not pleased the people we may be sure these political managers would not have presented them. In the early days there were no accessories to help a play along, no elaborate costumes, little stage setting, and no permanent seats for the spectators. The success of a performance depended solely on the popular qualities of the play itself and the skill with which it was presented. The Roman drama, therefore, reflected in a peculiar way the literary taste of the people, and the taste of the common people, too, because no charge was made for admission, so that ancient theatrical audiences, unlike ours, were not composed of the well-to-do, but of poor and rich alike. How discriminating was the literary judgment of the Roman populace in the second century B. C., the extant plays of Plautus and Terence bear witness. Indeed, Lucian Müller, the brilliant German critic, in his defence of the Roman audience, goes so far as to suggest a comparison of the literary merits of Roman comedies and of the plays which are put on the stage to-day, much to the disadvantage of the modern playwright. It is quite possible that a modern Plautus or a modern Terence would have some difficulty in finding a manager who would think it wise to stage his Rudens or his Andria. To the discriminating taste of the Roman populace must also be attributed the high degree of perfection to which the art of acting was brought by an Ambivius, a Roscius, and an Æsopus — a perfection of which such fine literary critics as Cicero and Quintilian speak with admiration. In our discussion we have confined our attention to comedy, partly for the sake of brevity, partly because no complete Roman tragedy of the early period has come down to us, and partly because comedy reflects in a peculiar way the taste of the people, but we should arrive at the same conclusion from a study of tragedy. Classical tragedies were put on the stage until the close of the Republic, and had a prominent place in the programme at the dramatic festival which Pompey gave at the dedication of his great theatre in 55 B. C.

But in the later days of the Republic legitimate drama was being crowded to the wall by the *togata*, the Atellan farce, and the mime. This change seems to indicate a decline of the popular taste, but perhaps it points not so much to a *decline*, as to a *change* in the taste of the people, and to the development of a new literary tendency. The comedies of Plautus and Terence portrayed Greek life; the scenes were laid in Greek cities, the actors wore a Greek dress, and the traditions, laws, and social practices upon which the plot rested were often foreign to Roman experience. The Roman wanted to see the life of his own time and of his own people represented on the stage. This craving found satisfaction in the three new forms of the drama which have just been mentioned. All of them dealt with the everyday life of the Italian people. In the mime, which proved to be the most popular of the three, this tendency toward realism found expression not only in the subjects which the playwright chose and in his method of presenting them, but in the great numbers of popular aphorisms which such writers as Publilius Syrus introduced into their plays, in attacks on contemporary politicians like those which Laberius made, in the giving up of masks and buskins, in the assignment of feminine rôles to women, and in the use of elaborate stage settings. The mime and the farce stood on a lower moral plane than comedy; but in their best literary form, as they came from the pen of a Laberius or a Publilius, they reached a high degree of development. In other words, the movement was away from idealism and toward realism. It is interesting, however, to note this fact in passing: that the interval of one hundred years which lies between the middle of the second and the first centuries before Christ is the period of political and social revolution; and that the triumph of realism over idealism, of the mime, who represents the masses in literature, over the tragic and comic actor coincides with the overthrow of the aristocracy by the democracy in the political world.

We have sought to estimate the literary taste of republican Rome by studying briefly the character of its drama. For the Romans under the Empire we shall try to find another test, but before doing so it may be interesting to supplement the evidence we have just found by asking ourselves with what Latin classics, outside of the drama, the Romans of the Republic and of the early Empire were most familiar. If Macaulay's New Zealander a thousand years hence can find out the English authors specified for admission to Princeton and to the other principal colleges of the Middle and New England States, he may not discover our favorite authors, but he will know those with whom we have some acquaintance. Similarly, if we know the school texts which the rising generation in republican Rome used, we shall know something of its literary range. Fortunately we can answer that question with some success. Roman literature begins with a schoolbook. The inspiration which impelled Livius Andronicus to translate the Odyssey came not from the Muses, but from his need of a text to use in teaching Latin to boys, and in reading the few extant lines of his work some of us may feel that they reveal the stiffness of the schoolmaster rather than the grace of the poet. Still Livius Andronicus deserves our sympathy and a certain measure of admiration even, for the Latin language in the middle of the third century before Christ was a rough instrument to use for literary purposes, and I am afraid we have the music of Homer's lines ringing too clearly in our ears to estimate the literary merits of his translator with fairness. But this Latin Odyssey was written for use in the schools, and that purpose it served faithfully, if not well, for two hundred years. Horace was brought up on it by "Orbilius of the rods," and his prejudiced estimate of early

Latin writers, even of Plautus, may be due in part to his trying experience with Andronicus and Orbilius.

Even the prosaic verses of Livius Andronicus seem almost touched with the divine afflatus when they are compared with the second text-book of whose use we hear. In his essay On the Laws, Cicero calls to his brother's mind the fact that they had both learned the Laws of the Twelve Tables in boyhood. It is needless to recall how unutterably barren these laws are, how harsh and crude, and how lacking they are even in broad legal principles. At all events, Roman boys and girls were not brought up on literary dainties. By the side of Livius Andronicus in the schools stood the national epics of Nævius and Ennius, to be supplanted in later years by the Æneid. Horace, too, in verification of his tragicomic apostrophe to his little book of Epistles as he sends it out into the world, fell into the hands of the village teacher, and in course of time Ovid and even Lucan and Statius underwent the same experience. No school-book, however, attained the vogue of the Æneid. On the walls of Pompeii, at the height of a school-boy's hand, one can read to-day rudely scratched copies of Arma virumque and Italiam fato. The other poets who are honored in the same place, but in less degree, are Lucretius, Ovid, Propertius, and Tibullus. The three last-mentioned authors probably enjoy a prominence on the walls somewhat out of proportion to their general popularity, because the quotations or adaptations of their verses which we find there seem to be made by lovers, who would come on more suitable sentiments in their writings than they would elsewhere. It is a noticeable thing that the favorite text-books were in verse. Of the prose writers only Sallust and Livy seem to have been used in the schools. Cicero, contrary to his own expectations as expressed in one of his speeches, was little read there. To make reasonably complete our list of the authors widely known we must add to these school-books the plays of Plautus, Cæcilius, Terence, Afranius, Publilius, Laberius, Ennius, Pacuvius, and Accius, with which the Romans, under the Republic at least, became acquainted in the theatre. Probably Roman schools would not be so important a factor in spreading a knowledge of literature as schools are in this country. The Romans of course knew nothing of compulsory education, and they had no organized system of state-supported schools; but even under the Republic the fees which private school teachers charged were so pitiably small that it must have been possible for children of the middle classes to get an elementary education. There is very fair evidence, too, from Pompeii and from what we know of certain arrangements made in the army that the average citizen could read and write. The election posters which we find on the walls of Pompeii, the tradesmen's signs, the announcements of articles lost and found, as well as the large number of jests and passing thoughts scratched on the stucco by loungers do not necessarily imply that the Pompeian was master of the art of reading to such an extent that he would enjoy an epic or a lyric poem, but they at least point to the conclusion that he could read. This state of literacy under the Empire need not surprise us when we recall the support which was given by many emperors to higher institutions of learning, and by many private citizens outside Rome to the elementary schools of their native towns. Pliny's generosity in helping to endow a school at Comum was not an isolated occurrence, as the benefactions recorded on the tombstones of generous citizens in various parts of the Empire abundantly testify. But could books be had by the average citizen? We think of the cheap book and the public library as blessings coming direct from the invention of the printing-press, and at first thought we may be inclined to suppose that in Rome, when copies had to be written by hand, books must have been as dear as they were during the Middle Ages when Bibles were chained to the desk. But of course we know that this was not the case. Copyists had been trained to attain such a speed in writing, and slave labor was so cheap, that in the first century of our era, as Martial tells us, the first book of his poems, which contains about seven hundred lines, could be had at a sum amounting to thirty or forty cents, while his Xenia could be sold for twenty cents. At these rates, books did not cost more than twice what they do to-day. But the people did not have to rely upon buying books. The fashion of founding public libraries, which was instituted by Pollio in the reign of Augustus, was taken up by other rich philanthropists in later days, so that by Hadrian's time there were no less than twenty-nine in Rome itself, to say nothing of collections of books in the public baths, and the practice adopted at the capital was probably followed in every considerable town throughout the Empire. This great chain of public libraries cannot have been intended to supply the needs of literary men or even of the well-to-do. It presupposes a very large reading public. Our conclusion therefore is for the Empire, as it was for the Republic, that the average Roman must have had a very fair acquaintance with his national literature, no longer through the medium of the stage, as had been the case in early days, but through attendance at the schools, through the multiplication of books at low prices, and through the establishment of public libraries.

In spite of all this evidence, I can imagine that doubt may still linger in some minds when the cruel amusements of the Roman people are recalled. Could a people who took such delight in gladiatorial contests find any pleasure in literature? Are brutal instincts and an æsthetic taste ever found together? I think in this connection we ought to remember the religious origin of the gladiatorial contests; we ought to remember that the people who took such a passionate delight in them had been accustomed to see them and to hear of them from infancy on, and came to regard them as the Spaniard looks at the bull-fight. We need only recall some of the great Renaissance patrons of art and literature to recognize the fact that cruelty and a capacity for æsthetic enjoyment may easily be found in the same character.

It occurred to me that we might learn something of the acquaintance which the common people had with literature by noticing the classical stories which are referred to in popular Latin literature. With that idea in mind I looked through some of the works of those authors who wrote for the masses or described their condition. The results were interesting, but out of the material I shall only venture to bring together a very few points from Plautus and Petronius, one a writer of the Republic, the other of the Empire. The evidence must be used with caution. The comedies of Plautus were adapted from the lost originals of Menander and Diphilus and Philemon, of course, so that we can rarely be certain whether a passage comes from the pen of Menander or Plautus. But Plautus treats his originals with considerable freedom, it will be remembered. He yields so far to his Roman audiences, for instance, as to insert references to contemporary men and things in the Greek setting of his plays. May we not, therefore, assume with probability that, in adapting the plays of Menander and Philemon for presentation to his countrymen, he would expunge from the lines of the Greek playwright those references to classical stories which would be unintelligible to his audience? This procedure would be much less violent than the opposite practice. It would not be destructive of the illusion, as mentioning contemporary events was, and the excision of such learned matter would be easy because it is generally introduced in metaphorical passages. At all events, let me mention a few of the classical myths which figure in tragic or epic poetry and are used by Plautus. We find Jason there, Bellerophon, Thetis, Ganymede, Phaon with whom Sappho fell in love, Philomela and the swallows, and, treated at some length, the stories of Hercules and of the Trojan War. I shall have to content myself with quoting a bit from a passage on the Trojan War. It will be remembered how frequently the slave in comedy, in plotting to get money from the old man, compares his enterprise to the storming of a city. That is the parallel which the slave Chrysalus has in mind in the Bacchides (v. 945 *ff.*), when he compares the soldier of the play to Menelaus, the young man Mnesilochus to Paris, the courtesan to Helen, and boastfully says: "To our stupid old man here, to him, I say, I give the name of Ilium. The soldier is Menelaus; I am Agamemnon, Ulysses, too, the son of Laertes; Mnesilochus is Alexander, who shall bring ruin to his home. He has carried off Helen, in whose behalf I am now laying siege to Ilium. Now I have heard in that very connection that Ulysses was, as I am, both bold and unscrupulous," and so he runs on for thirty lines until his soliloquy is interrupted by the sudden appearance on the stage of the old man who in the slave's exalted state of mind is Priam, the personification of Troy. If the average Roman citizen had not been familiar with the story of Troy it seems hardly probable that Plautus would have allowed this passage to stand in his play.

Petronius wrote his witty, cynical novel for his friends at the imperial court, but it is a picture of low life and in that respect is not uninstructive in this connection, for, at a dinner which the hero Encolpius attends, his host,

Trimalchio, a rich freedman, when somewhat in his cups, discourses upon several literary subjects and gives us his version of various classical myths. Among other topics he essays a comparison of Cicero and Publilius Syrus the mime. He tells his guests, too, that he has read Homer as a boy, and in illustration of his acquaintance with the poet recounts the origin of Corinthian bronze. It seems, according to Trimalchio, that "when Troy was captured, Hannibal, a sly fellow and a great rogue, heaped all the statues of bronze, of gold, and of silver into one pile and set fire to it; they were melted into one heterogeneous mass of bronze." He praises highly a bas-relief he has of Medea which shows, as he says, "how Cassandra kills her sons." The company at dinner is entertained by actors who present scenes from the Iliad, and Trimalchio gives a brief outline of the epic narrative, which in his version runs as follows: "Diomedes and Ganymede were two brothers. Their sister was Helen. Agamemnon carried her off. So now Homer tells how the Trojans and Parentini fight with each other. He won, of course, and gave his daughter Iphigenia in marriage to Achilles. That's the reason Ajax went mad." This doesn't speak well for the average man's acquaintance with classical myths, but perhaps Petronius has used his colors a little too freely in painting Trimalchio, and perhaps a present-day parvenu might not acquit himself better if he were asked to tell the story of King Arthur and the Round Table or relate the plot of Paradise Lost. We have spoken of libraries in the earlier part of this paper. Apparently the possession of books by a parvenu did not imply then, any more than it does now, the reading of them, for Trimalchio, as he tells us, had two libraries, one of Greek books, and one of Latin. The catholicity of his taste is illustrated by the fact that side by side on his walls were shown scenes from the Iliad and Odyssey and local gladiatorial contests.

And this brings us to the wall paintings at Pompeii. A large number of them deal with mythological subjects. We see among many others Priam turning back toward Troy with the ransomed body of Hector, Perseus and Andromeda looking at a reflection of the head of Medusa in a pool, Aphrodite caring for the wounded Adonis, Thetis in the workshop of Hephæstus, the young Hercules strangling the serpents, the fall of Icarus, and the sacrifice of Iphigenia. If only a few well-known classical incidents were depicted, we might suppose that they were traditional or conventional subjects whose appearance on the house walls would not necessarily imply the acquaintance of the householder or the artist with the underlying story; but their number and variety is really very great, as I have tried to show in the illustrations mentioned, and so many precise situations are portrayed that we must assume a rather intimate acquaintance with the legends involved on the part of the average Pompeian, and Pompeii is more instructive for us in this matter than Herculaneum would be, because it reflects the average culture of a prosperous Italian town.

While the Pompeian wall paintings point to an acquaintance with the subject-matter of epic poetry and tragedy on the part of the people, other evidence leads us to the conclusion that they were more or less familiar with the lines of some of the classical poets, or at least with popular sentiments from their works. An interesting study of the Roman metrical epitaphs was made a year or two ago by a German scholar for the purpose of finding out what the amateur authors of them borrowed from the classical poets. In them there were found some five hundred quotations or reminiscences from Latin authors. Virgil is here again the favorite poet, with Ovid and Lucan next in order. There is very little from Horace, now and then a reminiscence of Martial, Lucretius, Propertius, Tibullus, and Statius. However, in this case, as in discussing the quotations found on the walls of Pompeii, we ought to bear the fact in mind that a preference would naturally be shown for the poet whose sentiments would be most appropriate for the purpose in hand, and Horace wrote little that would be suitable for a tombstone.

These metrical inscriptions enable us to appreciate the taste of the Romans for literature on another and a more positive side. They, and the folk tales, constitute the literature which the common people have left us. Most of these poems are epitaphs. They were engraved upon stones placed along the highways which radiated from the great cities, and many of them were addressed to the passer-by. They come, then, from the average man and are intended for his eye. Almost two thousand of them have been preserved to us, and they run from the third century before Christ to the sixth century of our era. They present in an epitome the social history of Rome. At first we see only the native Italian stock represented in the names which they contain. Then gradually Greeks, Syrians, Celts, and all the other peoples whom Rome subdued. At first only distinguished men were honored in this way, but as the oligarchy gives way to democracy, the memory of all classes is perpetuated in verse, — nobles, commons, freedmen, and slaves. At first the stones record only noteworthy achievements in the field and in the forum; then come the virtues of private life, as the individualistic spirit makes itself felt. The development of industrial life is reflected in the epitaphs of workers in bronze, gold, and silver, of ship carpenters, and porters, of merchants, actors, and dancers. The simple faith of the early days gives way to the scepticism of the later Republic, to the Oriental cults of the Empire, and finally to Christianity. They take a tone of bravado, of resignation, of hope, or of doubt. They express a hope in a future life or they tell us that death ends all. Some of them warn us to be upright and virtuous, others to make the pursuit of pleasure the object of our lives. Had I a facile pen I should try to render a few of them into English verse, but I shall have to content myself with turning three or four of them into plain prose. A trader at Brundisium leaves this record of his life: "If it irks thee not, stranger, stop and read. On wingèd ships have I often hurried o'er the mighty deep; many lands have I visited; this is the end of my journeying which long ago, at my birth hour, the Parcæ foretold. Here have I left behind me all my cares and all my labors. Here I fear neither the heavens, nor the storm clouds, nor the savage sea. Here I fear not lest loss may overtop my gain. Kindly Faith, to thee I give my thanks, goddess most holy; thrice when fortune was broken and I in despair hast thou restored my fortune. Thou dost deserve that all men should yearn after thee. Stranger, mayst thou live, and fare thee well; may fate always bring thee gain since thou hast not scorned this stone."

Perhaps literature has not left us a truer picture of the Roman matron than has this stone from the Appian Way: "Stranger, what I have to say is quickly told; stop and read it to the end. Here is the unbeautiful tomb of a beautiful woman. Claudia was the name her parents gave her. Her husband she loved with her whole heart. Two sons she bore; of them the one she leaves on earth, the other she buried beneath the sod. Charming in discourse, gentle in mien, she kept the house, she made the wool. I have finished. Go thy way." A husband in his tribute to his wife writes: "Florentina, my sweet, sweet wife, sovereign mistress of my heart, modesty and purity and a loyalty which kept inviolate the marriage couch have made thee dear to thy husband. To the pursuit of arms have I been free to go with mind serene, and my household hath prospered under thy protecting care. Now thy desolate sons seek the comfort which thou didst give, and the house in sadness grieves when thou dost die." Near the town of Pisaurum was found the epitaph of a slave boy composed by his patron, who was also his father: "Traveller, thou who dost walk along the way with footstep firm, stop, I pray thee, and I beg thee, scorn not my epitaph. Twice six years and two months have I passed in the world above, tenderly cherished and loved. I have learned the doctrines of Pythagoras and the teachings of the wise, and I have read books; I have read the divine verses of Homer and the many rules of Euclid for the abacus. I had my pleasures, too, and boyish sports. (The honor of freedom) my father, who was my patron, would have granted to me, had I not unhappily suffered an adverse fate. But now a resting-place below — to the stream of Acheron, through the murky stars of bottomless Tartarus I go. I have escaped life with its unrest. Hope, beauty, farewell. With you I have no lot. Lead others on with your enticements, pray. This is my eternal home. Here have I been placed. Here shall I always be."

Four of the metrical epitaphs reveal to us a pleasing and unexpected side of Roman character. They are epitaphs on pet dogs. One was a great white hunting dog named Margarita who coursed through the trackless forests, as she tells us on her tombstone. Another "never barked without reason, but now he is silent." Myia, the little Gallic dog, barked fiercely if she found a rival lying in her mistress's lap. The stone of Patricus, an Italian dog, at Salernum contains this tribute from his mistress: "My eyes were wet with tears, our dear little dog, when I bore thee (to the grave), a service which I should have rendered thee with less grief three lustrums ago. So, Patricus, never again shalt thou give me a thousand kisses. Never again canst thou lie contentedly in my lap. In sadness have I buried thee, as thou deservest, in a resting-place of marble, and I have put thee for all time by the side of my shade. In thy qualities, sagacious thou wert like a human being. Ah me! what a loved companion have we lost! Thou, sweet Patricus, wert wont to come to our table, and in my lap to ask for bits in thy flattering way. It was thy way to lick with eager tongue the dish which oft my hands held up to thee, the whilst thy tail didst show thy joy." These translations reproduce very inadequately the sincerity, the delicacy of sentiment, the simple pictures of life, and the gracefully turned expressions which characterize some of these little poems. The construction of the verse they do not show at all. These half-dozen specimens of sepulchral verse are, of course, above the average of the great majority of metrical epitaphs. Many of the others are awkward, commonplace, and full of stock expressions, but those which have been given constitute only a small part of the really admirable bits of poetry to be found on tombstones and in dedicatory inscriptions. Now if we compare them with the obituary poetry and the sepulchral verse which the amateur poet of to-day writes, shall we not be inclined to reach the same conclusion concerning the comparative creative power of the Romans and ourselves which we reached with reference to their literary taste when compared with ours?

We set out with the purpose of finding out something about the literary taste of the common people of Rome and their acquaintance with literature, to see if the low esteem in which they are held in these matters is justified. We found in the drama a peculiarly satisfactory test of the literary appreciation of the Romans under the Republic, because plays were written for the masses, and we found that a higher standard was attained in these plays than is reached by the average play to-day. Under the Empire a knowledge of classical literature was spread in the schools which brought an elementary education within the reach of almost every one, and an acquaintance with good books was made possible through the production of cheap books and the establishment of many public libraries. We are not surprised, therefore, to find that the writings of popular authors and the Pompeian frescos presuppose some acquaintance on the part of the common people with the great classical myths and legends, and that the graffiti on the walls of Pompeii and the reminiscences of classical poets in the metrical epitaphs disclose a familiarity with many of the verses of popular authors. Finally, unnamed amateur poets have shown a creative power in the metrical epitaphs which goes far to confirm the favorable opinion which we have already been led to form by the other evidence of the appreciation which the common people of Rome had for literature and of their acquaintance with it.

THE CAREER OF A ROMAN STUDENT

IT is a remarkable fact that in the hot chase which historians for centuries have made after the minutest events of Cicero's life, the son, whose career might at least serve as a foil for the father's, has found no biographer. Yet it is quite possible to sketch the young man's career in some detail. In fact such a sketch takes an almost autobiographical form, since a large part of our information is drawn from the letters of young Cicero himself. From these letters and from those of his father, we get such a distinct impression of the young man's personality as few other characters of antiquity give us; while the escapades of the young Roman student, his promises of reform, and his pleas for more money, present, in outline, the true predecessor of the student of to-day.

Toward the close of the year 65 B. C., in a letter to his friend Atticus, the orator announces the birth of his son, the health of the mother, and the election of the new consuls in a single line, and after this curt announcement, turns to the news of the day. In addition to this strange grouping of items this letter is noteworthy also in introducing to us, perhaps for the first time, another prominent figure in Cicero's life, in the person of our old friend Catiline. The letter in question is, in fact, written to inform Atticus of Cicero's intention to undertake the defence of Catiline, and describes the rather questionable preparations which he and the other attorneys for the defence were making, while the son's birth receives but incidental mention. The circumstances attending the appearance of our hero upon the stage were, therefore, scarcely auspicious. In conformity with Roman custom, the boy received his father's name, Marcus Cicero.

An attractive boy, if we may accept the father's statement to his brother Quintus, "a son most lovable and dear to me," and precocious; for one thing which distressed Cicero when he was sent into exile a few years later was the knowledge that his son, although a boy of but seven, fully appreciated the disgrace and trouble which had come upon his father. His most intimate friend was his cousin Quintus. The two cousins, of almost the same age and of similar tastes, were brought up, in fact, as brothers; so that Cicero writes to Quintus the elder: "Your boy, who is the very image of you, my Cicero loves like a brother, and respects like an elder brother." The harmony which lasted to the end between the orator and his brother, interrupted perhaps but once, and then but for a moment, in the midst of political broils and civil wars which set father against son and husband against wife, was transmitted from father to son. This harmony was, in fact, considered of so much importance by the two brothers that not only were the boys brought up under the same instructors and in the same household, but even when the younger Marcus in later years urged his father to allow him to join Cæsar's army in Spain, Cicero was prevented from granting his request by the fear lest the favor which young Quintus had won with Cæsar might beget jealousy and ill-feeling between the two cousins.

Even amid the claims which politics and law made upon him, Cicero found time to take an active part in the education of his son, for, as he tells us in a letter to his brother: "I am writing this letter on the eighth day before the Kalends of November, the day of the games, while on my way to my villa at Tusculum, and I am taking young Cicero along with me to give him a taste of his books rather than of the circus"; and it may not have been a mere chance that the date of Cicero's departure from Rome coincided exactly with the date of the public games. The boy of eleven, like the young man of twenty, found more to satisfy his taste in the circus than in his father's study. At all events, the prudent father thought the atmosphere of Tusculum more suited to work than that of Rome.

Cicero's pamphlet of a few years later, De Partitione Oratoria, which is thrown into the form of a dialogue between him and his son, may well represent in an idealized form the intercourse between father and son upon these visits to Tusculum. Later events lead us to question very much the interest which the young man took in these philosophical discussions. As the two boys grew up, finding the personal attention which they required at his hands more than public matters would allow him to give, Cicero secured a private tutor for them in 56 B. C., and, probably following both his own judgment in the matter and the practice of his day, chose for that office a Greek named Tyrannio. The choice seems not to have been thoroughly satisfactory. At all events, in the summer of 54 B. C., to his great satisfaction, Cicero secured as their instructor Dionysius, a freedman of Atticus. The remarks which Cicero makes so frequently in his letters to Atticus upon the accomplishments of Dionysius afford a fairly good portrait of the man. Two thousand years have brought about little change in the lot of the private tutor. He was obliged to be then, as he must be now, a model of propriety, an encyclopædia of knowledge, and the willing slave of youthful whims. What the poor tutor suffered with his two rebellious pupils only those can picture whose lot has been a similar one. From 54 to the close of the year 50 B. C. Dionysius is mentioned as the constant companion and instructor of the boys. Even when Cicero was assigned to the proconsulship of Cilicia in 51 B. C., and took Marcus and Quintus with him, Dionysius went also, and carried on the education of the two boys mainly at the court of Deiotarus, while Cicero was engaged with the affairs of administration elsewhere. A Roman boy received the greater part of his education from his twelfth to his sixteenth year, and these were the years which young Marcus passed under the care of Dionysius. The two favorite text-books in Latin in Cicero's day were the Laws of the Twelve Tables for prose, and for poetry the translation of the Odyssey by Livius Andronicus. The bald style and dry contents of the one and the wooden character of the other, may well excite our sympathy for the young man in his struggles with his mother tongue. Cicero would scarcely allow his son to slight his study of the Twelve Tables, which, he tells us in the De Legibus II, 9, he learned by heart in his boyhood, because he hoped that young Marcus might follow in his footsteps as a lawyer. So far as Greek was concerned, Cicero had been warned in his youth by experienced friends that a liberal education must include a thorough knowledge of it. We may be sure, therefore, that he took pains to lay emphasis upon that side of his son's instruction, and the young man must have mastered the language, for, some years later, as we shall presently see, we find him living in Greece and attending lectures given in Greek.

The ominous silence which Cicero maintains during these four years concerning the literary progress of the son, upon whom he based such fond hopes, is in striking contrast to the freedom with which he chats with his friend Atticus upon all other matters, personal and political—a silence which is broken by only one utterance of any significance, and that occurs in a letter from Laodicea, which bears the date of February, 50 B. C., when young Marcus was fifteen years of age. In writing of the progress of the two boys Cicero says: "They are fond of each other, they study together and take their exercise together; but one of them, like Isocrates in Ephorus and Theopompus, needs the curb; the other, the spur." Although Cicero did not at the time reveal to us which one of the two required the spur and which one the curb, the future was to do it. A passage in the same letter shows us that the boys began to chafe under the rule of the schoolmaster; and it is not strange, on the other hand, that the temper of even the philosophic Dionysius should have given way now and then under the strain, so that, as Cicero writes, "the boys say he is awfully cross," a phrase whose pathetic extravagance vouches for the fact that it comes from the lips of the boys themselves.

In Laodicea young Quintus assumed the *toga virilis* and with it, doubtless, a distaste for further academic pursuits. To lose the better pupil of the two was too much for the patience of Dionysius, and upon reaching Italian soil he left Cicero to go back to the service of Atticus. Cicero's efforts to induce him to return to his charge were of no avail, and in the end the father fell into such a bad temper over the matter, that of the man whom he had before styled "not merely a learned man but also a very conscientious one, who is desirous of my approval, and is upright, and, not to praise a freedman, a man in the best sense of the word," he writes, "by my soul, you would think I was asking a Dicæarchus or an Aristoxenus to return, and not a person who is the worst chatterbox in the world without any aptitude for teaching." In accordance with Roman practice, young Marcus might hope with the assumption of the *toga pura* upon March seventeenth in 49, to turn his back forever upon philosophy and law, and devote himself to the profession of arms, toward which his tastes had long led him.

The moment was certainly an auspicious one for a young man of good family with military aspirations. Upon this very seventeenth of March, Pompey, driven from Italian soil by the vigor of Cæsar's movements, had landed at Dyrrachium in Greece, and either leader was more than willing in face of the coming struggle to accept the help of any young man of promise. Young Marcus, who cared little for political considerations, would have preferred to fight by the side of the young and active Cæsar rather than with the older and over-cautious Pompey, while his father's practical neutrality during the civil war makes it quite probable that he would have kept his son in the same attitude which he himself took, had he been able. The compromise between father and son upon this point resulted in the young man's enlistment under the banner of Pompey, where, as commander of a squadron of cavalry, he won golden opinions from both general and army by his skill in riding, throwing the lance, and by his powers of endurance. But in the very passage in which Cicero refers with pride to his son's success in arms, when he adds, "successes which we win by the use of our intellect and reasoning power are more gratifying than those which come from physical excellence," it is easy to see that the father's ambition would not be satisfied by military achievements, no matter how brilliant they might be. He could not give up the hope that his son should seek his fortune at home rather than in the field. The battle of Pharsalus in 48 B. C. put an end to the military hopes of young Marcus, who returned once more to Italy and waited with his father to see what turn events would take.

The coldness which had sprung up between his father and mother led, some time during the year 46, to their divorce, and Cicero's marriage to his young ward, Publilia, soon followed — a turn of affairs which seems to have been unbearable to the son. Young Marcus, therefore, presented to his father the choice between two alternatives, either that he should be established in a house of his own at Rome or should be allowed to join Cæsar in Spain. Cicero in writing to Atticus quotes the young man's words: "He wants to go to Spain or to have a liberal allowance;" and the laconic way in which the youth of nineteen puts the matter indicates plainly his determination to start out in the world for himself. We may imagine how distasteful both of these propositions were to Cicero: either that his only son should publicly cut loose from him and set up an establishment of his own, or that he should follow the standard of Cæsar, who had overthrown Cicero's political party and exterminated its leaders, who had exalted his enemies, the "*improbi,*" and wrecked his political influence. He decided at last that the latter was the lesser evil of the two and consented to his son's departure for Spain, while evidently casting about for some escape from this unpleasant arrangement. The aedileship of Arpinum offered such an escape. It will be remembered that Arpinum was Cicero's native town, and the pride which the Arpinates took in their illustrious townsman knew no bounds, so that the candidacy of young Marcus doubtless went through with a rush. It is unfortunate that Cicero gives us no account of the political canvass. The picture of the campaign from his pen would be a highly interesting one. Young Marcus possessed all the qualities of a successful "practical politician." He was doubtless a big, powerful fellow, noted as we know for his athletic accomplishments, devoted to "sport," with the reputation of being able to stand more strong drink than any man in Italy, a jolly companion, and an enemy to the "kid-gloved" aristocracy. Less can be said, perhaps, of his qualifications for this office of Commissioner of Public Works, but in practical politics this was a minor question then as it is now. He could at least run well. His colleague in the aedileship was his cousin Quintus. We may fancy that Cicero intended this position to be the first step in his son's political career, with the consulship at Rome for the ultimate goal; but the future had in store for him a plan even more to his taste, for at the close of his son's term of office Cicero's long-cherished hope that Marcus might continue his studies, which had been broken off by the untimely departure of Dionysius, was brought nearer to realization by the plan which he announces to Atticus in the latter part of the year 46. This plan was nothing less than that the young man should go to Athens, and complete his education at the University there, as the noble scions of so many Roman houses were already doing.

Cicero's daughter, Tullia, died toward the end of February, 45 B. C. Her death was the culminating point in a long series of misfortunes which came upon him in rapid succession within a period of twelve months — the divorce of his wife, Terentia, the separation from his second wife, Publilia, his quarrel with Quintus, the coldness between himself and his son, so that from the depths of his despondency he writes in the Tusculan Disputations: "Deprived as I am of my political honors and of my home life, what hope has the future left for me? Would that I were dead!" It implies, therefore, an immense deal of self-sacrifice upon his part that, in the moment of his loneliness and despondency, he could not only consent to the departure of his son, but could even make arrangements for his stay at the University. It was only, in fact, a few weeks after Tullia's death, when Marcus set out for Athens. On his way thither he fell in with a fellow student, L. Tullius Montanus, and became so warmly attached to him that, to gratify his son's generous impulses, Cicero paid a debt of twenty-five thousand sesterces which stood against young Montanus. The lively picture which Capes in his Oxford lectures gives us of student life in Athens at a later day, can hardly represent in all its details the state of things in Cicero's time; but, as young men have been the same the world over, the practices which prevailed in the second and third centuries A. D. probably existed, in their germ at least, in student circles at Athens at the beginning of our era.

Let us hope, however, that our young Roman freshman did not meet with so warm a reception as was accorded a newcomer in later days. Capes quotes from the reminiscences of such an one as follows: "Most of the young enthusiasts for learning, noble and low-born alike, become mad partisans of their professors. As those who have a passionate love of racing can hardly contain themselves, but copy all the gestures of the jockeys, or bet upon the horses entered for the prize although they hardly have the wherewithal to live themselves; so the students show their eagerness for their teachers and the masters of their favorite studies; they are all anxiety to get their audience larger, and to have their fees increased. And this is carried to portentous lengths. They post themselves over the city, on the highways, about the harbor, on the tops of the hills, nay, in lonely spots; they win over the inhabitants to join their faction. As each newcomer disembarks, he falls into their hands; they carry him off at once to the house of some countryman or friend who is bent on trumpeting the praises of his own professor, and by that means gaining his favor or exemption from his fees." A graphic but pathetic picture of student life from another point of view is quoted in the words of one of the professors himself: "I send my slave out to all my scholars to summon them to lecture, and he starts off at a run to do my bidding. But they are in no mood, like him, to hurry, though they ought to be even more in haste. They stay, some of them, to sing their songs, which we have all heard till we are tired, or else they amuse themselves with foolish merriment and jesting. If their friends or bystanders remark on their delay, and at last they make their mind up to be off, they talk about their sweethearts as they go, or on the skill of some dancer at the circus, and they gossip even when they get inside, to the annoyance of real students. This they do until the lecture has begun. And even when the subject is being discussed, and explanation is going on, they keep whispering to each other about the jockeys and the races, or some comedians and opera dancers; or about some scuffle past or future. Meantime some of them stand like statues, with their arms folded on each other; others go on blowing their noses with both hands; others sit stock still, unmoved by any of my strokes of brilliancy or wit. Some try to interrupt those who do feel stirred. Others vacantly cast up the numbers in the room or stare at the trees that grow outside. . . . I had a different set of pupils once. . . . Each of them used to carry away something in his memory of what I said, and then they would put their heads together and compare notes, and write my speech out fair. They were quite distressed if they lost any of the heads, although that seldom happened. . . . But as for you, you can only tell inquirers that I have been lecturing, but cannot repeat a word of what was said."

But to return to our hero. Inasmuch as Cicero was absent from Rome the greater part of the year 45, he authorized Atticus, who had trusty correspondents in Athens, to make all necessary financial arrangements for his son's sojourn abroad. To meet the running expenses of his university course, Cicero set apart the rental from a house upon the Aventine and certain shops in the Argiletum. The snug sum which resulted therefrom would seem to have been sufficient for a student of modest tastes, but the tastes of Marcus were evidently not of the modest sort, for he pathetically writes home in regard to his teacher, Bruttius, "I have hired a place for him near by, and I help him out in his poverty so far as I can from my own scanty means," and it was found necessary to eke out the young man's allowance by the payment of additional sums now and then, payments which the prudent Atticus was less willing to make than Cicero. The orator's unwise generosity toward his son was occasioned not merely by paternal fondness, but also by a hope that through a lavish expenditure of money his son might make himself popular with his fellow students and gain access to the more exclusive circles of Athenian society, as may be gathered from his letter to Atticus at the moment of his son's departure: "I shall take care that neither Bibulus nor Acidinus nor Messalla, who I understand will be at Athens, shall have more money to spend than he (Marcus) gets from these rentals." In this hope father and son were disappointed. The young Bibulus and Messalla at Athens frowned upon the social aspirations of the younger Marcus, as their fathers at Rome had frowned upon those of the elder, and the only intimate friends of whom mention is made are the freedman's son Montanus and the renegade rhetorician Gorgias. And what was still more unfortunate, the father's generosity caused the son's demoralization. On sending his son to Athens, Cicero had requested one of his college instructors, Leonides by name, to keep a watchful eye upon the young man and now and then to report progress to him. Much to the disgust of young Marcus, the letters of Leonides were of a very frank nature and unfortunately agreed only too well with the private advices which Atticus received of the young man's proceedings. Marcus could evidently pass a better judgment upon a bottle of wine than upon a system of philosophy, and he spent more time in the "kneipe" than in the lecture room, although doubtless Pliny's story is somewhat extravagant that young Cicero could swallow twelve pints of wine at a draught, and that he thus took poetic justice upon Mark Antony, his father's future enemy, by robbing him of his reputation of being the hardest drinker of his time. The boon companion of Marcus upon these occasions was his teacher of rhetoric, Gorgias. Cicero was in a high state of indignation when the reports of this fact reached his ears, and ordered the dismissal of the recreant tutor at once.

This was the condition of things in December of 44 B. C., when Marcus wrote the letter which has been preserved to us by the recipient Tiro. The character of the honest freedman Tiro, and his relations to Cicero, are well known. He was Cicero's Boswell, preserving as priceless treasures the letters and even the jests of the orator. It was, therefore, a politic stroke on the part of young Marcus to address this sheet of good resolutions for the future to his father's kind-hearted secretary and confidant, who would know the right time, and the method of approaching his father. In a condensed form, the letter would read somewhat as follows: "It is a long time, I confess, since I have written to you, but I have really been waiting for a letter from you, which has only just reached me after having been forty-six days on the way. The delight which both your letter and my father's gave me more than repaid me for waiting. I have no doubt that the better reports concerning me were gratifying to you. I assure you that you may become the champion of my reputation with a clear conscience. The errors of my past conduct cause me so much sorrow, that not only do I now shudder at the thought of such things, but my very ears burn at the mention of them. I have become not merely the pupil but the son of Cratippus. I spend whole days and nights with him. As for Bruttius I do not let him depart from me. I have, in fact, hired apartments for him next door, and help him out as far as I can from my scanty means (*ex meis angustiis*). Besides that I have lessons in Greek declamation with Cassius, and in Latin with Bruttius. My most intimate friends are the learned men whom Cratippus brought with him from Mytilene. I found Gorgias useful for declamation, but as my father asked me to dismiss him, I did so at once. So you have bought a farm. I am very glad to hear it. I can imagine you buying farming tools, and talking with the overseer. By the way, I wish you would send me a secretary,—a Greek I prefer; I lose much time in copying lectures. Take good care of your health, so that we may have literary discussions together by and by."

The epistle is delightfully frank, and politic at the same moment — frank in its statements of affection for Tiro and of regret for the past, politic in its account of that past and its good resolutions for the future. It is a student's letter *par excellence*, with its excuses for neglect in writing home, its anxiety to appease an angry father, its regret for the past, its glowing account of work at the present, its brilliant literary hopes for the future, its solicitude for the health of the recipient. Even a suggestion of financial difficulties and a hint for further advances find a place in it. Change the scene from Athens to Princeton or Cambridge, the date from B. C. to A. D., the name to Robinson or Brown, and the student's letter of to-day is complete.

The kind-hearted Tiro would not hesitate to accept at their face value the young man's protestations, and to plead the writer's cause before his master. In fact, a letter to Cicero from Trebonius, who visited Marcus at the university at this time, vouches for the honesty of his resolutions; but this literary activity which filled the young man's nights as well as days was brought rudely to an end by the news which came from Rome in March of 44 B. C. Their social sympathies, their courses of study, the liberal instincts of youth, with a host of other influences, combined to make enthusiastic republicans of the Roman students at Athens, and it needed only the tidings of Cæsar's death to convert them into active supporters of the republican cause. The call to arms drowned in their ears the milder exhortations of philosophy. One of the first to join the ranks of Brutus was the young Cicero. Under his standard the young man showed the same soldierly qualities which had distinguished him in the Pompeian War. No more gratifying words could reach the ears of Cicero than these of Brutus himself: "Your son Cicero, by his activity, his painstaking care, his devotion to work, and his broad-mindedness, indeed, by the manifestation of every good quality, makes such a favorable impression on me that in point of fact he never seems to forget whose son he is."

It will always cause regret though not astonishment to the student of literary history, that young Cicero and Horace, although fellow-students, were never brought into contact with each other at Athens. It would be delightful to know the impressions which Horace, the hard student, and Marcus, the ne'er-do-well, had formed of each other, but we search for them in vain. The gulf which lay between them in the student world was impassable. It is, however, strange — when both, of nearly the same age, enlisted at the same place and time, and held the same rank under the same commander, — that Horace at least does not mention his companion in arms. With the death of his father in December of 43 B. C., our knowledge of young Cicero's movements comes nearly to an end. In the pages of Seneca and Pliny, the career of our hero serves merely to point a moral or to act as a peg upon which to hang an historical statement. His political harmlessness saved the son from the fate which had overtaken the father. There can be little doubt that Marcus joined the party of Octavianus rather than that of Antony. He was in fact the man who brought back to Rome the first news of Antony's defeat; and, partly in return for his services, but still more in repentant recognition of his father's merits, Octavianus made Marcus, in the young man's thirty-fifth year, his colleague in the consulship for the latter part of the year 30 B. C. It was left for the son to avenge upon Mark Antony the death of his father, for it was the senate, presided over by the young Cicero as consul, which removed the statues erected in Antony's honor, took from Antony his titles, and declared that none of his descendants should bear the name of Marcus. As Plutarch puts it: "So fate intrusted to the household of Cicero the last act in the punishment of Antony."

Young Cicero disappears from the stage as the proconsul of Asia, and as an epitaph upon the careless, jolly Roman student stands the stately official inscription lately found at Aquinum, and dedicated by the people of that town to their patron:

[1] M(*arco*) Tullio M(*arci*) f(*ilio*) M(*arci*) n(*epoti*)
M(*arci*) p(*ro*) n(*epoti*) Cor(*nelia tribu*) | Cic-
eroni co(*n*) s(*uli*) proco(*n*)s(*uli*) prov-
(*inciæ*) Asiæ leg(*ato*) Imp(*era-*
toris) | Cæs(*aris*) Aug(*usti*)
in Syria | patrono.

[1] To Marcus Tullius Cicero, of the Cornelian tribe, son of Marcus, grandson of Marcus, great-grandson of Marcus, consul, proconsul of the province of Asia, legate of the Emperor Cæsar Augustus in Syria. To their patron.

SOME SPURIOUS INSCRIPTIONS AND THEIR AUTHORS

SEVERAL scholars in modern times have written chapters on literary forgery, but no one seems to have studied in a comprehensive way epigraphical forgery and the methods which are employed in detecting it, although there is no field of classical study in which dishonesty has brought such confusion as in epigraphy, and, on the other hand, in no investigations have scholars displayed more acuteness than they have shown in detecting spurious inscriptions. This paper, however, does not aim to give a complete survey of the subject. Its purpose is merely to bring together a sufficient body of facts from the notes in the Corpus of Latin Inscriptions and from the reports of scholars in the epigraphical journals to show the development of the art, and to illustrate the methods of some of its most famous, or infamous, promoters.

It was so easy two or three centuries ago to compose an important inscription, and to win distinction by publishing it to the world, and so difficult to detect its spurious character, that many scholars yielded to the temptation. Furthermore, the opportune publication of a forged inscription might save a weary search in establishing a point, furnish a missing link in a chain of evidence, or administer a *coup de grace* to a stubborn opponent. In view of this situation we are not surprised to find that the number of spurious or suspected inscriptions mounts up to 10,576 in a total of 144,044, corresponding to a ratio of about one spurious to thirteen authentic inscriptions. The condition of things in the several volumes of the Corpus varies greatly. Against vol. VII, with only 24 spurious and 1,355 authentic inscriptions, stand vols. IX and X, which cover the old kingdom of Naples, with totals for the two volumes of 1,854 [1] and 14,841, which stand to each other in the ratio of one to eight. Since each volume of the Corpus contains the inscrip-

[1] These numbers represent the inscriptions published up to the present time in vols. II–XIV of the Corpus Inscriptionum Latinarum. Vol. I is not included because the inscriptions contained in it are republished elsewhere, and Vol. XV is excluded from the calculation because the spurious inscriptions have not yet been published for that volume. For our purpose it is also unnecessary to take into consideration the published inscriptions which have not yet been included in the CIL.

tions found in a particular part of the Roman world, one covering Spain, for instance, and another the city of Rome, these differences between the several volumes in the matter of forged inscriptions, of which the cases just cited are characteristic, tempt one to an estimate of the comparative honesty of the Spanish, Roman, Neapolitan, French, or English epigraphist and antiquarian. Two or three independent facts also seem to indicate that the national standards in this matter among the several European peoples have not been the same. Thus, for instance, Donius, an epigraphist of the seventeenth century, fresh from the chagrin which his deceitful amanuensis Grata had caused him, writes to a friend expressing a desire for a Belgian to fill the position of secretary for him "because Italians as a rule are little suited for such a post" (*cf.* CIL,[1] VI, 5, p. 228*), and Borghesi was so indignant at the large number of forgeries from Naples that he was inclined to hold all Neapolitan inscriptions under suspicion. On the other hand, the Englishman may feel some national pride in the fact that only twenty-four spurious inscriptions are found in the collection from Britain. But

[1] The Corpus Inscriptionum Latinarum.

conclusions based on national or geographical considerations must be drawn with great care, for, in point of fact, all the principal continental peoples of Europe — the Italians, the Germans, the French, and the Spanish — have had representatives in the art of forgery, and an examination of the spurious inscriptions shows that the composition of them is characteristic of a particular period rather than of a given region. The publication of fictitious inscriptions goes back to the fifteenth century and was practised as late as the middle of the last century, but its Augustan age runs from the middle of the sixteenth to the middle of the seventeenth century. Since Italy furnished the most fruitful field for epigraphical study at that time, as it does to-day, and since, consequently, Italians outnumbered others in cultivating it, it is not strange that Italian forgeries are more numerous than those from other sources. It is also true, as we shall have occasion to notice, that two or three Italian scholars were very prolific in this field and, therefore, have brought up the national average. Turning from the geographical factor to the time element, perhaps we should not boast too much, at the expense of our predecessors, of the higher standard of epigraphical morals which prevails now, because the certainty of detection exerts a most salutary deterrent influence upon those who might be inclined to sin in this matter to-day. We have now a systematic collection of inscriptions; critical principles are well established, and interest in classical antiquities is so general and all parts of the Roman world are reached to-day with such comparative ease, that a forgery, or the attribution of a forged inscription to a particular place, would be readily detected.

Felix Felicianus of Verona, of the fifteenth century, who is perhaps best known for an interesting little treatise upon the letters of the alphabet and the best methods of drawing them (*cf.* R. Schöne in Eph. Epigr. I, p. 255 *ff.*), may, perhaps, be regarded as the father of epigraphical forgery. The art did not appear in its completed form at once, and the earliest practice of it was comparatively naïve and harmless. Felicianus and his immediate successors never, or rarely, forged inscriptions outright, but they pretended to find in some ruin an inscription mentioned by an ancient author, or their fictitious finds were based upon some statement found in literature.

Thus Michael Ferrarinus reports as one of his discoveries the epitaph of the poet Ennius, obviously taking the text from Cicero's Tusculan Disputations, i, 34, and Mazochius in his Epigrammata Antiqua Urbis, published in 1521, reports the following inscription: Divo Gordiano victori Persarum, victori Gothorum, victori Sarmatarum, depulsori Romanorum seditionum, victori Germanorum, sed non victori Philipporum (CIL. VI, 5, I * S). This is, of course, taken bodily from the life of the three Gordians (chap. 34) by Julius Capitolinus. The latest-known forgeries are those of Chabassière, a French engineer who in 1866 published through the Academy of Constantine several African inscriptions, one of which, an inscription of King Hiempsal, was recognized as a forgery by both Mommsen and Wilmanns (*cf*. CIL. VIII, p. 489), and cast discredit upon all the other inscriptions reported by Chabassière alone.

If the Berlin Academy had persisted in following up the plan, which it had adopted in 1850 at Zumpt's suggestion, of basing the Corpus mainly upon the epigraphical texts given in manuscript and printed collections, probably most of the spurious inscriptions which have been composed during the four centuries which intervene between Felicianus and Chabassière, and which now languish under the dreaded star affixed to them by the editors of the Corpus, would never have been thus stigmatized. Fortunately Mommsen, before publishing an inscription, insisted upon examining the stone, whenever it was in existence, and demonstrated the feasibility of his plan and the correctness of his method in his Inscriptiones Regni Neapolitani, which appeared in 1852. Fortunately, too, Mommsen had, perhaps unwittingly, selected for this first scientific collection a field, viz., the kingdom of Naples, where forgers, as we noticed above, had been most active. The attention of the editors of the Corpus was thus drawn at the outset to the importance of detecting forged and interpolated inscriptions, and many of the critical principles upon which the science rests to-day were formulated and applied by Mommsen in this preliminary work (*cf.*, *e. g.*, CIL. IX, p. xi). From this early period comes, for instance, the well-known classification of all previous collectors in three categories: (1) the honest and careful; (2) the dishonest, and (3) the negligent, credulous, or ignorant. The principle of classification adopted for the second group is Calvinistic in its severity. One demonstrated lapse from honesty on the part of a collector condemns every inscription for which the scholar in question is our only direct source of information. To prevent any spurious inscription from slipping into our collection, the adoption of this principle was undoubtedly necessary, but the pessimistic view of human nature which it suggests does not correspond to our every-day observation of life. A man may turn aside from the truth once or twice, but may, in the main, follow the path of rectitude, and the sweeping character of this critical rule is probably responsible for putting many authentic inscriptions in the suspected list, and some cases of this sort have already come to light (*cf.* CIL. VI, 5, pp. 253 *–55 *). It would seem desirable soon to examine these lists in the several volumes systematically in the light of new discoveries and of our increased knowledge, in the hope of rescuing authentic inscriptions from their present position among the suspected or condemned. That the principle underlying the second grouping of collectors does not lean toward lenity seems to be indicated also by the fact that no inscription regarded by the editors of the Corpus as authentic has been condemned later.

The most prolific forgers in the period from Felicianus to Chabassière were Boissard, Gutenstein, Ligorio, Lupoli, Roselli, and Trigueros. The names — French, German, Italian, and Spanish — indicate, as observed above, that scholars of all the principal continental countries were guilty of this offence. The devious methods of Francisco Roselli are especially hard to follow because he at the same time forged some inscriptions and copied many other authentic ones, but copied them carelessly. His collection, which was made up partly of inscriptions from Grumentum, was published in 1790, and Mommsen, finding it very difficult to make a correct estimate of his work from the published collection, went to Grumentum in 1846 to study his method of procedure. He found that the people of Grumentum regarded Roselli as their most distinguished citizen, and they gave their visitor all the help they could to make the fame of their fellow townsman known as widely as possible. Mommsen's embarrassment when he discovered the true character of Roselli and had to publish the facts is best indicated in his own words (CIL. X, p. 28): "I hope that the good people of Grumentum, who have helped me in my investigations, and whom I cherish in grateful and loving remembrance, may not be angry at me because I have spoken frankly about Roselli, and have wished to be honest rather than complaisant." Among other peculiarities Roselli's MS. shows some very interesting afterthoughts. In one case (CIL. X, 43 *) he forged an inscription in honor of a certain Q. Attius in which the people of his native town were characterized as Bruttii, but, finding later that they were really of Lucanian origin, he revised his inscription by dropping out the line in which the Bruttian origin was mentioned.

Roselli's purpose was apparently to bring distinction to himself and his native town. Gutenstein's motive was more altruistic. He was Gruter's amanuensis and not only reported authentic inscriptions to his master, but also forged others to gratify Gruter's intense desire for additions to his collection. Many of his inscriptions he pretended to have found in the collections of Metellus and Smetius. His dishonesty was discovered when these collections were examined and Gutenstein's inscriptions were not found among them (*cf.* CIL. VI, 5, 3226*–3239*; Bormann Eph. Epigr. III, p. 72). His epigraphical style is well illustrated by Mommsen in Eph. Epigr., I, pp. 67–75. One of the inscriptions there quoted is in honor of Septimius Severus. Another reads as follows: DDD.[1] nnn. | Valentiniano Valenti et | Gratiano Auggg | piis felicibus ac | semper triumfator. | signum Herculi vict. | ob prov . . . | rect . . . | ampli . . . votis X | . . . is xx. On these two Mommsen remarks (p. 68): "the titles and the repetitions of them in the first inscription the reader will explain as easily as he will fit a cap to the (triple headed) Geryon; in the second one the juxtaposition of the three emperors of Christianity pure and undefiled, and of the statue of Hercules the Victor is like the appearance of the sun and moon in the sky at the same time."

The method of Lupoli, a bishop at Venusia, was to take inscriptions from the collections of Gruter and Fabretti, add a few genuine ones of his own, and forge others to complete

[1] "To our masters, Valentinian, Valens, and Gratian, the emperors gracious, favored by fortune, and always victorious, a statue to Hercules the Victor, etc."

his collection. His work is characterized by the stern indignation which he expresses at the inaccuracy and dishonesty of other epigraphists.

In the Rh. Mus. XVII (1862), pp. 228 *ff*., Hübner tells in a graphic way how he unmasked Trigueros. The conduct of the Spanish epigraphist was peculiarly and ingeniously perfidious, because he attributed his own forged inscriptions to a scholar of a previous generation who was probably a creation of his own imagination. He had already taken a similar course in the case of a piece of literature forged by him, so that this method of procedure must have appealed to his malicious sense of humor.

But the prince of forgers was the Neapolitan Pirro Ligorio of the sixteenth century. In a burst of indignant admiration de Rossi characterizes him (Inscr. Chr. Urbis Romæ, p. xvii *) as "that brilliant maker and inventor of deceptions." Ligorio held a very distinguished position among the scholars and artists of his day, was the friend of Smetius, Pighius, and Panvinius, and succeeded Michelangelo in supervising the work at St. Peter's. The Vatican library has twelve manuscript volumes from his hand, the Barberini ten, and the library at Turin, at least up to the time of the late injury to that collection by fire, thirty more. Of the 3,643 spurious inscriptions which CIL. VI, pt. 5, contains, 2,995 emanate from Ligorio. His audacity is incredible. Many of his forgeries he pretended to have found in the gardens or libraries of well-known houses in Rome (*cf.* CIL. VI, pt. 1, p. lii, col. 1), and as a rule he mentions the exact location, *e. g.*, he locates VI, 1460 * "dentro la chiesa di San Nicola di Cavalieri in via Florida presso della Calcare." Sometimes he gives an airy description of the supposed monument, as in describing a monument, the inscription upon which is published in CIL. VI, 1463,* he says: "Upon it one sees the likeness of the Gorgon, and about the Gorgon on the right and left hand two butterflies seem to flit. It has also a festoon of fruit." Sometimes he based his productions on a single authentic inscription (*cf.* VI, 1819 * and VI, 1409); sometimes he combined two authentic inscriptions (*cf.* VI, 1866 * and VI, 1739, 1764), but more frequently he forged outright. His versatility in the matter of content and form is extraordinary. He treats a great variety of subjects, combines Greek and Latin (*e. g.*, VI, 1653 *), composes a fragmentary inscription (*e. g.*, VI, 1665 *), imitates the illiterate, as in using the form *ongentarius* (VI, 2066 *), and indulges in such paleographical novelties as ligatures (*e. g.*, VI, 1657 *) or heart-shaped separation points (*e. g.*, VI, 2079 *). He carried his work even to the point of carving more than one hundred of his forgeries on stone, most of them for the museum of his patron the Cardinal of Carpi. Some of these have been discussed by Henzen in Comm. in Hon. Mommseni, p. 627 *ff.* His inscriptions had been suspected by a number of scholars, but their spurious character was first clearly shown by Olivieri at a meeting of a learned society in Ravenna in 1764 (*cf.* Inscr. Lat. Sel., ed. Orelli, I, pp. 43–54).

Most of the prolific epigraphical forgers have some idiosyncrasies or some stylistic peculiarities, or they are ignorant in some specific field of the Latin language or of Roman life, and these weaknesses not infrequently betray them. Gutenstein, for instance, in copying an inscription from a previous collector, had the strange habit of making some slight change in a title or a date, as Mommsen has shown in

Eph. Epigr. I, p. 71. Thus, for example, he changes *pietatis Imperatoris Cæsaris* to *pietati et felicitati imp. Cæs.*, and May 13 appears in his copy as February 8, although it is impossible to see why he made the alteration. Ligorio's tendencies and the points at which he is ignorant are brought out very clearly by Henzen in Comm. in Hon. Mommseni, pp. 627 *ff*. He is weak in the syntax of the cases and not infrequently puts the accusative after the preposition *a* or *ab;* he is not familiar with the Roman system of nomenclature and, consequently, confuses *nomina* and *cognomina*, gives a slave a *nomen*, or adds *servus* to the name of a freedman. His two fads are to put an apex over the preposition *á*, and to coin titles of the type *á potione*, to which he is prone to add a word that changes altogether the meaning of these stereotyped expressions; cases in point are *faber á Corinthis*, and *á balnea custos*. The editors of the Corpus have studied the stylistic characteristics of these two men with such care that Mommsen (*op. cit.*, p. 75) can say with truth: "The man who is familiar with the art will distinguish the work of Gutenstein from that of Ligorio as unerringly and with as little trouble as those who have devoted themselves to the study of the Latin poets distinguish the lines of Virgil from those of Ovid."

The true character of most of the forgeries was not discovered until long after they had been made. In the mean time they were copied into new collections by scholars all over the world, who often failed to indicate the source from which they had borrowed, and one of the most laborious tasks which the editors of the Corpus have had to perform is in tracing an inscription back through manuscript and printed collections to a Lupoli or a Ligorio. Thus VI, 2942,* forged by Ligorio, was borrowed by Panvinius, taken from him by Donius, and finally found its way into Muratori. Not infrequently forgers have been deceived by the inventions of other forgers. Ruggieri published IX, 180 * from Mirabella. In the fourth line of Ruggieri's copy stood *prov. apuliae.* The unscrupulous Pratilli took the inscription from Ruggieri, but changed the two words mentioned to *proc. apuliae,* and finally Lupoli in his collection edited *proc. apuliae,* but later without comment changed the reading to *corr. apuliae.* The motive which actuated most forgers was a desire to win distinction by the number or importance of their discoveries; some of them wished to prove a point, or to establish the antiquity of their own families. This last motive accounts for Lupoli's invention of IX, 157,* which makes the Roman Lupulus his ancestor: C. Bæbius Lu | pulus. et C. Bæbius Lupul. f | Silvano. deo | vot. s. l. m.

It may not be out of place to give a few of the spurious inscriptions which are most interesting in themselves or show a feeling for the picturesque or a sense of humor on the part of the forger. The monument which Hannibal set up on the field of Cannæ for Paulus Æmilius, the Roman leader, bore this epitaph: "Hannibal did not suffer the body of Paulus Æmilius, the consul of the Romans slain at Cannæ, to lie unburied, but he sought it out; with the greatest honor he intrusted it to the Roman soldiers to be placed beneath this marble and his bones he had transported to Rome," IX, 99.* This is the passport which Cæsar gave Cicero: "We, Gaius Cæsar, decree that Marcus Tullius Cicero, because of his extraordinary virtues and his surpassing mental gifts, go safe and unharmed anywhere through the world brought into subjection by our valor and arms," VI, 81.* We should have no hesitation in assigning this inscription to September 47 B. C., and we owe its anonymous composer a debt of gratitude for bringing up in so concrete a way the memory of that dramatic meeting of the conqueror and the conquered at Tarentum or Brundisium, at the close of a long year of anxious and frightened waiting — a meeting of which no other record has survived. The inscription, however, whose spurious character we admit with the greatest reluctance is VI, 3403,* which purports to contain fragments, eleven in all, from the Acta Diurna, or The Day's Doings, of the second and first centuries before our era. The composition seems to go back to the close of the sixteenth century, and is perhaps to be traced to Ludovicus Vives (*cf.* Heinze De Spuriis Actorum Diurnorum Fragmentis). It passed unquestioned through the hands of a number of distinguished scholars, Lipsius, Pighius, Camerarius, Grævius, and Vossius, and its authenticity was vigorously defended as late as the middle of the last century. It aroused the special interest of British scholars. John Locke called the attention of Grævius to it about the end of the seventeenth century, and

Dodwell devoted himself particularly to its explanation and defence. How cleverly it was composed, so far as content goes, and how valuable it would be, were it authentic, may be illustrated by an extract from the year 168 B. C.: "On the fourth day before the Kalends of April, it was the turn of Licinius to exercise consular power; there was a flash of lightning and a thunder-bolt and an oak on the top of the Velian Hill was struck a little after midday; there was a brawl in a tavern near the arch of Janus, and a tavern-keeper at the sign of the Helmeted Bear was badly injured; Gaius Titinius, the food inspector, fined the butchers because they had publicly sold meat not inspected; from the fine a shrine was erected at the temple of Tellus Laverna." This whole composition, in fact, is the *chef-d'œuvre* of the epigraphical forger's art, and reminds one of the missing chapters of Petronius which Nodot cleverly composed and gave to the world a century later, and the true lover of antiquity will almost feel inclined to resent that blindness to the picturesque on the part of the historical critic which has robbed us of this unique specimen of a Roman daily newspaper.

THE EVOLUTION OF THE MODERN FORMS OF THE LETTERS OF OUR ALPHABET

IT has often seemed to me that the study of the art of writing *an und für sich*, of pure paleography as opposed to applied paleography, if one may use those expressions to indicate two different methods of investigating the art of writing, is sadly neglected. This will be apparent, I think, if we call to mind the end or ends toward which our study of paleography is directed, and the work which we actually do in this field. Our first object in pursuing the subject is to learn how to expand abbreviations and to read the common scripts —this for the purpose of acquiring some facility in simply reading an original MS. Then we study the shapes which the several letters, or combinations of letters, take in different periods and countries; we examine the scribal practices of different schools in the matter of using initials and ornaments, and we learn something about the history of ink, papyrus, parchment, and paper, about the division of the page into columns, and about other similar matters, so that, when we take up a MS., we may form an intelligent opinion on the question when and where it was written. We try to acquire some acuteness in distinguishing different inks and the hands of different correctors; in diagnosing the scribal weaknesses and the besetting sins of a given copyist; in noting the points at which he has evidently gone astray, either on account of his own ignorance of Latin or his unfamiliarity with the script which he was copying, or because the text before him was illegible. Our purpose here, of course, is to get back as near as possible to his archetype — to the text which he was trying to follow.

The same process, some steps only of which have been here indicated, we follow with another MS., and then another, until we have covered all those which are available. Thereupon we make a comparative survey of them all; we reject those MSS. which are worthless for the purpose in hand; we arrange the rest in family groups on the basis of common ancestry, and we determine the comparative value of the several families and the members of each family. From these results we proceed to reconstruct a text which shall represent as nearly as possible that left by Cicero or Livy.

All this is necessary, and one may freely recognize the fact that the primary value of paleography lies, and should lie, in its use in restoring a text, but it is unfortunate that we should stop at this point in our study of it. It is unfortunate that we should give almost all our attention to the study of applied paleography, and very, very little to the investigation of pure paleography. We have handbooks and collections of facsimiles which give us this working knowledge of the science of writing which I have described above; the introductions to our classical texts and our classical journals give us collations of MSS. and papers based upon the application of paleography to difficult passages in a text; but one very rarely sees discussions of paleographical questions dissociated from their practical application in restoring a text, and yet as a pure science paleography furnishes a discipline which in some respects can hardly be excelled.

Furthermore, handwriting in its development, like all the other arts, reflects the temper and tastes of a period, the characteristics of a race, a nation, a school of learning, or an individual, in a most illuminating fashion. We study every other art historically and for its intrinsic value, and we consider the art of a given period as an expression of the temper of the times. In other words, we study its development in the light of contemporary social and political history. The art of writing has not the importance for us which literature or pictorial art or architecture has, but it has an independent value, and deserves to be studied for itself; and the method of study which is applied to the other arts is equally applicable in this field. In the case of paleography, when a script is so novel in form, or when a change in style is so extraordinary that it challenges even a languid attention, we may stop for a minute to consider its historical setting. The script of Tours for instance, by its extraordinary beauty and symmetry, or later Roman cursive or Merovingian texts by their complex awkwardness, may call so loudly for an explanation of their existence that we make some effort to find one; but we rarely stop to consider how the social or political changes of a period, or the characteristics of a nation or a race, are reflected in handwriting, or to ask ourselves through what stages *ARMAVIRVMQVE* developed into *arma virumque*, and how and why the successive changes took place.

We rarely bring the script of the *Aufschriften* into vital relation with that of the *Inschriften*, or try to estimate the influence of the book hand and the diplomatic hand upon each other. Our study of the three scripts is carried only to the point where it will be of service in reading and interpreting inscriptions, classical manuscripts, and documents, respectively.

To come back to what was said before, we content ourselves with the bare facts of paleography, in so far as they are of practical use in text reconstruction. The case would be the same in the field of syntax, if we contented ourselves with such a knowledge of the inflectional forms and their meanings as would enable us to read Greek, Latin, or German, but took no interest in finding out how one syntactical relation developed out of another. Syntax, like paleography, is of most value for the service which it renders in another field than its own, but that fact does not by any means rob historical syntax or historical paleography of its own peculiar and independent interest; and the mere arrangement of phenomena in the correct chronological order, which is all that our treatises on paleography attempt, does not make the study of that subject historical any more than a similar method of studying grammatical constructions constitutes historical syntax.

This is a long introduction for a short paper, but it may be excused in part by the fact that one of the purposes of the paper is to illustrate the value of pure paleography by a brief and modest excursus into that field.

The point which I wish to present in it is that in the development of writing the working of the principles of evolution is shown more fully and more simply than in any one of the biological sciences, and that proposition I should like to illustrate from the history of certain letters. The letters which have been selected for the purpose are: A, B, D, G, H, N, Q, and R. It will be most convenient to begin with Q, because the development of that letter is simplest.

The theory of evolution as applied to biology starts with the fact that, given a single species at the outset, nature tends to produce in course of time new representatives of that species which differ slightly from the original type. This is exactly what happened in the evolution of the letter Q. The form which we find in the earliest Latin inscriptions is a circle, or an oval approaching very closely to a circle, with a tangential affix drawn horizontally to the right from the bottom of the circle ( ). This primitive type threw off as variants the three main varieties , , and . The first two of these gave rise to the subvarieties and , in which the tail was in some cases so prolonged as to extend under three or four of the letters to the right.

Let us look first at those modifications of these early descendants in which the point of contact between the affix and the circumference of the ellipse was pushed along the base of the curve toward the left. Out of variant No. 1 developed a form in which the pendant was drawn downward, viz., , and this form gave rise to such modifications as , , and , and ultimately to what is essentially a new type, , with the affix drawn downward to the left. From the second variant there were no important derivatives. Variant No. 3 became one of the accepted forms of the initial, and gave rise to our capital , so called. Next to stands , in which the stroke has reached the lower left-hand corner of the oval. This is the farthest point to which it went in its progress to the left.

Now let us return to the original type, , and follow the affix in its advance in the opposite direction, that is, upward along the circumference. We find the pendant first starting at various points between the base-line and the top of the circle, and , until finally it reached the top of the circle in the typical form , which, in turn, threw off a number of subvarieties, , , , , . and I ought to say in passing that all of these forms have been arranged, not in chronological order, but in the order of development; that is, an attempt has been made to connect each form with its immediate graphical ancestor, so to speak, and not with the form which happens to precede it chronologically in extant inscriptions or manuscripts. In this way, although the ends of the series, like or , in which the stroke starts from the left-hand side and is perpendicular, or in which the circle has become essentially a horizontal line, seem very far removed from the primitive form , the connecting links make the line of descent apparent. I have ventured to say above that the working of the Darwinian principles is shown more clearly and more intelligibly in the development of writing than in the field of biology. This statement is substantiated, it seems to me, by interpreting the facts which we have just noted. The biologist accepts the variation of species as a scientific truth, but he can offer no adequate explanation of it. The factors which come into play are so many and so elusive, and the possible combinations of them so numerous, that finite intelligence cannot yet, at least, take them all into account. In dealing with the development of writing the cause of the variation is reasonably clear. These graphical variants which we have been examining are the intended productions of the individual copyist. They reflect his temperament, or a conscious purpose or an unconscious tendency on his part. If you push the investigation a step farther back, and ask why he had such a temperament, or showed a given desire, or followed a certain tendency, we cannot give a complete answer, and yet, as our investigation proceeds, I think we shall be able to find the motives which controlled his action, and so gave rise to the development of all these forms. Thus far we have seen how the first great principle, the tendency to vary the original type, worked itself out in the development of the letter Q.

The second truth established by Darwin and others in this connection is that, given an original type and several varieties, that variety or those varieties which are fittest to survive *will* survive. What factors determine the fitness to survive of a graphical form? They are in the main legibility, beauty, economy of effort, and economy of space. In one set of circumstances it is one of these factors, in different circumstances it is another, which exerts the preponderant influence, and determines the character of the resultant form, just as in the animate world one variety is best adapted to survive in one environment and another variety meets better a different set of requirements. The slave, or the monk, who is copying an edition of Horace for the Mæcenas of his time, will pay little heed to economy of effort or space, but will aim to secure beauty and legibility. When he comes to the initials at the beginning of the books or at the tops of the pages, he will sacrifice even legibility, and show an utter disregard of time and space, so to speak, so that, assuming the general character of the symbol to be fixed, the only efficient motive which influences the copyist will be a desire to produce a beautiful or symmetrical letter. With the clerk who is transcribing a *senatus consultum* for the archives, or the engraver who is cutting it in bronze, legibility will probably be the controlling consideration. The lounger, on the other hand, who is scratching a sentiment on the outer wall of a Pompeian house, will sacrifice beauty, legibility, and space to his desire to save himself trouble.

The free play of these four controlling motives was hindered or facilitated by tradition and by the use of one material or another. The reverence for the Bible and for Virgil was so great, for instance, that a copyist felt himself almost compelled to adopt one of the noncursive hands, like the square capital or uncial, and use the approved forms of the letters of these alphabets. As for the different materials, bronze allows more freedom of movement than stone, wax surpasses bronze in this respect, and letters can be *painted* on a hard surface with still greater ease. The freedom of movement which one of these materials allowed when compared with another found expression in the reduction of angles to curves, in the failure to follow a fixed type closely in forming a letter, and in the comparative disregard of uniformity within a document. If we take almost any pair of inscriptions, of an early date, found in the same place, and equally formal in character, one of which, however, is engraved on stone and the other on bronze, we can observe all three of the differences noted above. The bronze tablet will very likely show the curvilinear ϵ in place of the rectangular E of the stone. It may offer a T composed of two wavy instead of two straight lines, as required by the strict-capital type. In it we are likely to find both the capital M and the uncial ɱ. The interrelation of the epigraphical and the manuscript hands has not been fully recognized and sufficiently studied. In one respect, in particular, the influence which the script used on permanent material had upon the book-hand has been misunderstood, as it seems to me. We commonly assume that the letters cut by an engraver in stone will be more angular than those drawn by a copyist on papyrus, and, therefore, we naturally conclude that the influence of the epigraphical script will make for angularity. Yet it is doubtful if this assumption is true for all cases. In point of fact, there is considerable reason for believing that at a comparatively early period under the Empire the letters of an inscription were commonly outlined on the surface of the stone with a brush. The introduction of this practice would have the effect of reducing angles to loops, and the influence of the epigraphical script upon the book-hand in such cases would be away from rather than toward angularity.

If we compare the two materials which were commonly used for literary purposes, papyrus and parchment, we shall find that the surface texture of a sheet of papyrus was nearly the same over the entire piece, but that on parchment a stroke of the pen in one direction was with the grain, while in the opposite direction it was against it. As the letters of the alphabet in their evolution, other things being equal, followed the line of least resistance, on *a priori* grounds we should expect to find that the peculiarity, just noted, of the surface of parchment would act as a restraining influence on the free development of the papyrus script; or, to put it in another way, since parchment drove out papyrus, we should not be surprised to see the line of development which the letters followed during the papyrus period turn aside, when the new material came into common use. This fact will be illustrated later in specific cases.

To pass to another point, some materials are comparatively cheap, so that in using them economy of space is not an important consideration. We shall expect to find, for instance, greater lateral extension in the script used on papyrus, or on paper, than on parchment. In so far as economy of effort is concerned, the practice of employing monks as copyists introduced an unusual economic factor, because in most cases the prior or abbot set them to work, not primarily for the sake of reproducing the classics, but in order to save the monks themselves from idleness. *Individual* copyists in the monasteries may have been careless and hasty in their work, but a desire to save labor was not an active influence with those who *directed* the work. It would be interesting to follow out in detail some of these modifying influences, and to trace their effects in the development of the various scripts, but that would take us too far from our immediate purpose, and, after all, the primary factors which have determined the general trend of development, and without which secondary agencies, like the influence of tradition, or the cost and the character of the material used, would have had no effect at all, are the four factors mentioned above, viz., legibility, beauty, economy of effort, and of space. It is also true that in ordinary writing the form which satisfies best in their order of importance these four requirements will survive, and this brings us again to the second dogma in the doctrine of evolution.

With the secondary influences in mind which we have just been discussing, let us return to the scribal "sports" of *Q* to see which of them meet best the four requirements mentioned above, and which are consequently the fittest to survive in every-day use, taking up first economy of effort. In estimating the comparative ease with which the various forms of Q could be made it is necessary to bear in mind the fact, already noted, that the alphabet was developed in its later stages on parchment, that upward strokes on this material are against the grain, that the pen would not move smoothly in that direction, and that consequently those forms could be most easily made which were composed of downward strokes readily drawn. In a well-known capital text of Virgil of the sixth century, preserved in the Vatican, the letter is clearly made with three strokes, .[1] The form probably has the same number. Perhaps and are painted forms only, but, had they been made on parchment, they would probably have required three and four strokes, respectively. Forms ordinarily made by the copyist in two strokes, as can be seen in the MSS., were , , , , , , , and .[2] In the facility with which they could be made, then, the forms of the second group had an advantage over those of the first. Most of them could also be readily joined to preceding and following letters when writing became continuous. When paper, whose surface is equally smooth in all directions, came into use, the advantage of the second group of forms was still greater, because they could be drawn by a continuous stroke, without taking the pen off. Even at an early period, on papyrus whose surface resembles that of paper, the

[1] The strokes are left unjoined to show the method of formation.

[2] The forms , , and are probably not found on parchment, and may be left out of consideration here.

single-stroke letter appears, since a fragment of one of the Herculanean rolls offers the form [letter form] . When the one-stroke letter comes in, [letter form] would be likely to drop out of the competition, because the pen must change its direction in adding the affix. Another factor, as we shall presently see, eliminated it before this influence made itself felt. The types which meet the test of economy of effort are, therefore, [letter forms], and [letter form], with its carelessly finished variants [letter form] and [letter form].

Let us now examine the various forms of *Q* from the point of view of legibility, beauty, and economy of space. The original type [letter form] is open to the objection that if the horizontal stroke is very short, it is hard to distinguish the letter from O, for a letter to be legible must be not only simple in form, but also easily distinguished from other letters. The objection on this score to [letter form] with a short affix becomes still greater when the letters, to save space, are reduced to minuscule size. The form [letter form] may well have failed of acceptance for the same reason, that is, because of its likeness to O, especially in the minuscule size. Then, too, it would require great care to insert the affix. To return to the type [letter form] , if the horizontal stroke is a long one, it occupies too much space. The difficulties which we have just discussed stood in the way of the adoption of q, q, q, q, q and q. The forms p and p are illegible because they are likely to be confused with p (*i. e.*, with the letter which follows o). The forms q, q, and q would be rejected because they are unbeautiful and unsymmetrical. The shape q is also unattractive. As for q, it is legible, but it lacks grace, and it does not stand firmly on the base line. We are left with q, q, and q. Of these three forms, which are variants from the same type, the second requires less space than the first, and it stands more firmly on the base line. For these reasons it has the same advantage over the first form that the b, d, f, h, l, and p, made with a perpendicular downward stroke, have over the forms of these letters which are drawn with a slanting stroke. The form q has a slight advantage over q, whether the latter be made with a closed or open loop, in that, when it is joined to a following letter (qr), it is easily distinguished from gr, whereas q, so connected (gr), is almost indistinguishable from it. The form q has then an advantage over all the others in its economy of space, its symmetry, and legibility, and at the same time, as we have tried to show above, it is one of the shapes which is most easily made and connected with letters preceding and following it. It has the four qualities required in a letter, and is, therefore, the one most likely to triumph, as it actually does triumph, over all its rivals. This form was readily adapted to use in a continuously written hand by drawing a stroke from the bottom of the letter to the next letter, thus, [illegible].

Now, in the process of evolution in the biological world, certain animal or plant types which have been crowded out by some other type or types often survive on some island where they have not been brought into competition with the prevailing species, or in some environment for which they are better fitted than their otherwise favored competitors. So the variants [illegible], [illegible], [illegible], and [illegible], while losing in the struggle for a place in the body of the text, found islands of refuge in the initial or capital position. In fact, the novelty of their shapes as compared with that of the form regularly used, and their adaptability for decorative purposes made them fitter to survive in these positions than the accepted minuscule form. Their struggle for existence even in these favored localities is still going on and there are some indications that in handwriting at least they may disappear altogether. q made large, for instance, not infrequently appears as a capital.

The working out of the principles of evolution can be traced in the development of each of the letters in the same way as we have traced it in the case of the letter Q, but a detailed examination of them is unnecessary. If the different forms of the several letters be arranged in the order of development, the process of evolution and the controlling influence of the four factors above mentioned will be apparent. The process by which the capital letters C, E, F, I, K, L, M, O, P, S, T, and V have developed into their commonly accepted written and printed minuscule forms can be made clear by a few words of comment. If the capital, the printed and cursive minuscule forms C c *c*, K k *k*, O o *o*, P p *p*, S s *s* be placed side by side, it is evident that the printed minuscules have been derived from the capitals by a mere reduction in size, and that the cursives differ from the former only in consequence of the slight modifications which are needed in attaching them to the letters which precede or follow them in continuous writing. In the case of E e *e*, F f *f*, M m *m*, and V u *u* there has been a change in size and a reduction of angles to curves. L l *l*, T t *t* show the reduction in size and an abbreviation of the horizontal stroke. The dot over the small form i was probably placed there to distinguish ii from u. The history of A, B, D, G, H, N, and R in their development into a, b, d, g, h, n, and r is not so apparent. Consequently we shall need to make a fuller study of this group.

The principal varieties of A resulted from the different positions given to the horizontal stroke and from the variation in length of one or the other of the upright strokes. Some of the typical forms of this letter in the capital script are [forms of A], and [form of A]. The one which, with a slight modification, proved to be the fittest to survive was the last of the series shown here, viz., [form of A]. This form could be made in two strokes, and that it was so made is clear enough from the MSS.[1] It

[1] *Cf.*, for instance, ZANGEMEISTER AND WATTENBACH, *Exempla, etc.*, No. 17.

involved an upward stroke, it is true, but this difficulty was minimized by making that stroke very light, or by going part way back on the short downward stroke. This led to a thickening of the line at the bottom of the short downward stroke and facilitated the substitution of a loop for the acute angle at that point. Now, by developing the long right-hand straight line into a curved stroke, the copyist made the letter more symmetrical, made it stand more firmly on the base line, and the modern printed minuscule a was obtained, which readily became ɑ in a continuously written hand through the desire to save labor.[1]

The development of H was similar. The position of the horizontal stroke and the relative lengths of the upright strokes are again the varying elements, and the forms H, H, H, H, H, H, H, and H result. The successful type developed out of the last form. This, as it stands, requires three independent strokes. If, however, the right-hand upright be terminated at the horizontal stroke, and the right angle made by those two

[1] It is interesting to notice that ɑ appears sporadically (*cf.* Z. & W., 31, of the seventh or eighth century), while the a was still in the process of development.

strokes be converted into a curve, h h, we obtain a letter which may be made without taking the pen off — a letter which is also symmetrical, similar in character to the other approved letters, legible, and economical of space.

The development of N follows that of H so closely that it needs no comment. The minuscule d comes merely from an effort to economize labor, and to bring the shape of the letter into harmony with b and h — , D ,),), d , d . d

An examination of the Pompeian graffiti and of the inscriptions painted on the walls of Pompeii seems to indicate that B was ordinarily formed in this way: the perpendicular stroke was drawn from above down to the base line. Then the lower arc was formed immediately, without removing the pen, and without returning to the top of the perpendicular, as we ordinarily do to-day in forming capital B, so-called. Then the upper arc was formed. The careless writer, however, failed to finish the upper curve, and we find at an early period such forms as B and b, until finally the upper arc dropped away altogether — b. The slight modification (b) which this form required for convenient use in a continuous cursive script is apparent without comment. If, in making B, we draw the arcs first, another development is possible, viz., , , ,[1] and this last form, which is actually found in Pompeii, had, perhaps, the history indicated, but it could not survive because of its similarity to d (D).

The printed form g seems far removed from G, but the connection between the two is established by this series: , , , , , , , , g; or by this one: , , , . I need not say that all of these forms, as, in fact, all of those given in this paper, except the two forms of b assumed above, actually occur in inscriptions or MSS. The governing factor in the last case seems to have been legibility. The cursive g has of course come from the prolongation of the affix and the closing of the arc — , , . With the closure of the arc it was necessary to throw the downward stroke back — thus, — to distinguish it from q.

The significant stages in the development of printed r are , , , and . The controlling factor here is the same as that which

[1] I have found only the first and last forms of this series. The second and third are suggested as possible connecting links between the others.

prevailed in the case of B, viz., a desire to economize effort. The genesis of ꝛ is evident (R, R, ꝛ, ꝛ, ꝛ). In the development of this cursive form the elimination of the perpendicular stroke was facilitated by the fact that R was frequently combined with O into a ligature in the many Latin words ending in or, and in this ligature the same line served as the right-hand semi-ellipse of O and the upright of R.

It would be interesting to stop and consider what parts of the Roman Empire furnished the most favorable environment for the production of these graphical "sports" and in what periods they flourished in the greatest number and variety, but such an investigation is reserved for a subsequent paper. I cannot bring this discussion to an end, however, without noting the fact that the development of the art of writing has been due in the first instance to the careless, the eccentric, and the hasty scribe — to the lounger at Pompeii, to the boy on his way home from school, who stopped to scratch the alphabet on the wall, and to the careless accountant, secretary, or monastic copyist. *They* dared to originate forms which the engraver or the trained copyist would never have thought of inventing, or have dared to introduce. They were the true reformers in whose footsteps *longo intervallo* the professional scribe timidly followed.

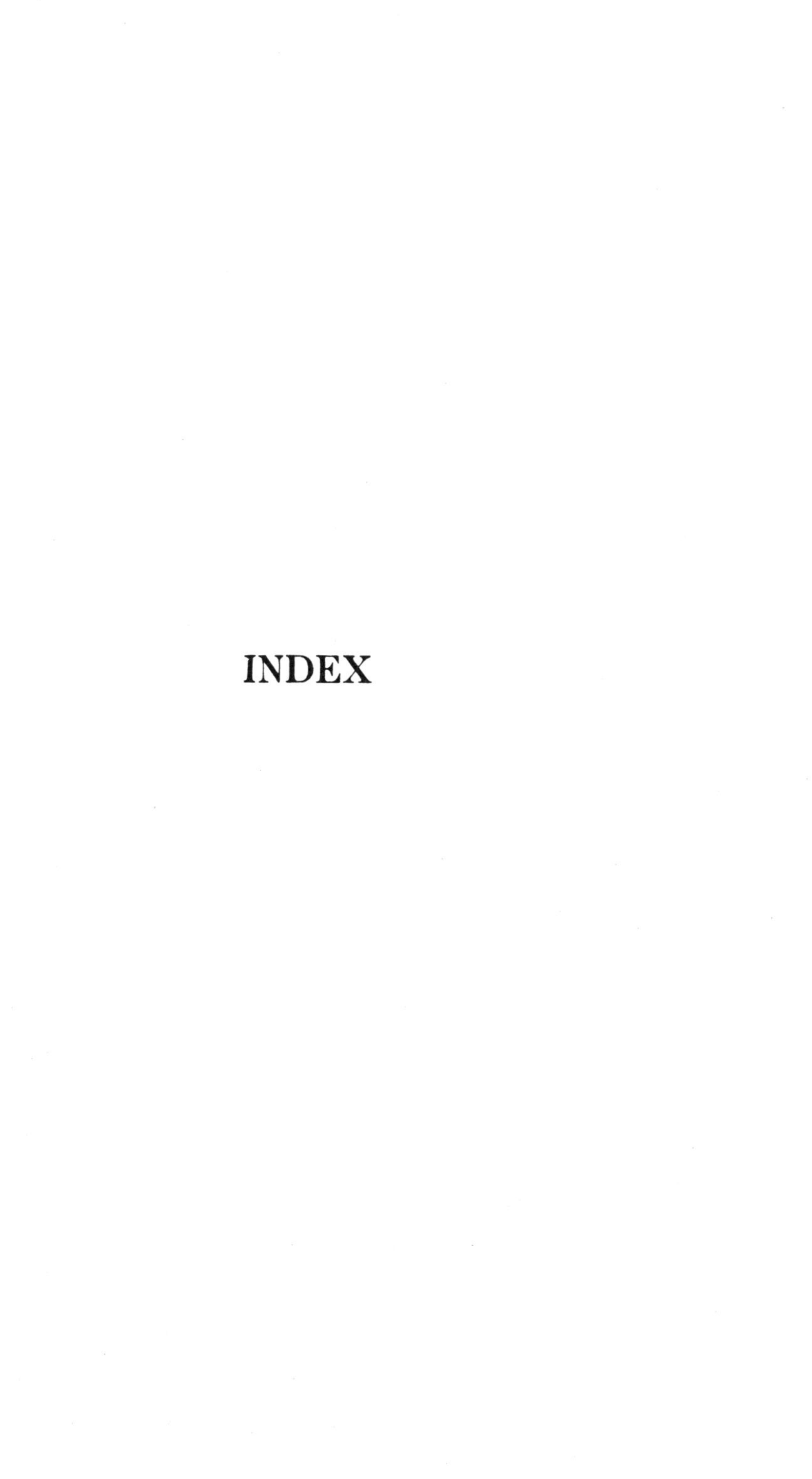

INDEX

INDEX

A, the development of the letter, 254–5.
Aetheria, the "Pilgrimage" of, 93–5.
Agnodice, the woman physician, 79.
Agrippina, the "Memoirs" of, 91–3.
Androgyne; her own lawyer, 84–5.
Antony and Fulvia, 74–6.
Assemblies, Roman popular, their character, 102–3.

B, the development of the letter, 256–7.
Books, cost of, 175; school books, 170–3, 196.

C, the development of the letter, 253–4.
Cæsar, his political marriages, 59; relations with Pompeia, 59; with Servilia, 67–9.
Cato the Censor and women in politics, 46–7.
Chabassière's forgeries, 220.
Charters, municipal, 3 *n.*, 19.
Cicero and Clodia, 55–8; and Servilia, 68–71; Cicero on "Candidacy for the Consulship," 106; his extant works in Petrarch's day, 156–7; his "De Partitione Oratoria," 194; his despondency in 45 B. C., 202–3. (See also *Cicero the Younger, M.*)
Cicero the Younger, M., his birth recorded, 191–2; relations with his cousin, 192–3; early education, 193–6; dislike for study, 197–8; he reaches manhood, 198; desires to be a soldier, 199–200; effect on him of his father's second marriage, 200–1; aedile at Arpinum, 201–2; goes to Athens to study, 202–3; not successful socially, 206–8; inclined to be dissolute, 208–9; his letter of repentance, 209; not acquainted with Horace, 212–3; avenges his father, 214; his epitaph, 214.
Claudia's epitaph, 42.
Cleopatra's policy, 61–3.
Clodia, her appearance and character, 55–6; Clodia and Catullus, 55; and Cælius, 56; and Cicero, 56–8; Clodia and the revolution, 58.
Clodius and Fulvia, 72–3.
Common people of Rome, the, regarded as philistines, 160–2; their literary taste tested by comedy, 164–8; by tragedy, 168; by the mime, 168–170; their school-books, 170–3; their school training, 173–4; their ability to read 174–5; to buy cheap books, 175; to use libraries, 175–6; their acquaintance

with classical stories as shown in Plautus, 177–9; in Petronius, 179–181; in wall-paintings, 181–3; their literary productions, 183–9.

Consulship, the Roman, lack of continuity, 32–3; subordinated to the senate, 34, 36–7.

Conventus matronarum, the, 50–1.

Cornelia and the revolution, 53–4; her "Letters," 90–1.

Curio and Fulvia, 73–4.

D, the development of the letter, 256.

Dionysius, a Roman tutor, 195, 197–8.

Drama, the Roman, 164–9; the popularity of Plautus and Terence, 164–7; the prologues of the Hecyra, 165; ancient and modern comedy compared, 167; Roman actors, 168; popularity of tragedy, 168; development of realism, 168–170; the mime, 169; classical stories in Plautus, 177–9.

E, the development of the letter, 253–4.

Education, Roman, at Athens, 203–6, 210. (See also *Books*, *Cicero the Younger, M.*, and *Schools.*)

Egeria, 44.

Electoral methods, 6; interference by central government, 11; conditions in Rome under the Republic, 103–5; use of force, 103–4; bribery, 104–5; disorder at public meetings, 105; political demonstrations, 105. (See also *Political Posters.*)

Eucharis, the solo singer, 96.

F, the development of the letter, 253–4.

Felicianus, the epigraphical forger, 219.

Ferrarinus, the epigraphical forger, 220.

Fulvia's character, 72; Fulvia and Clodius, 72–3; Fulvia and Curio, 73–4; Fulvia and Antony, 74–6; she takes control after Cæsar's death, 74; her mastery of Italy, 75.

G, the development of the letter, 257.

Gutenstein, the epigraphical forger, 224.

H, the development of the letter, 255–6.

Hersilia, 44.

Historians inclined to contrast and systematize, 160–1.

Horace and Persius, 140–3.

Horatia, 43.

Hortensia, 49.

House of Representatives, the, its loss of prestige, 22–4; its relations with the Senate, 24–5.

Hyginus's "Fabulæ," 78.

I, the development of the letter, 253–4.

Inscriptions, varied character of the metrical, 183–5; specimens, 185–8; estimate of them, 188–9; large number of spurious inscriptions, 216; their geographical distribution, 216–8; their time distribution, 218; early forgers, 219–220; the latest forger, 220; critical principles, 221–3; famous forgers, 223–8; their weak points, 228–231; some famous forgeries, 231–3. (See also *Political Posters.*)

Julia and Pompey, 59–60; her political influence, 60.

K, the development of the letter, 253–4.

L, the development of the letter, 253–4.
Law, the Oppian, 45–8; Laws of the Twelve Tables, 172. (See also *Women.*)
Libraries, Roman public, 175–6.
Ligorio, Pirro, the epigraphical forger, 226–8.
Literature, influence of women on literary form, 87, 122; on style, 88; their slight productions, 89–90; the better-known women writers, 90–5.
Livia and Octavianus, 76.
Livius Andronicus, 171–2.
Lucretia, 43.
Lupoli, the epigraphical forger, 225–6.

M, the development of the letter, 253–4.
Malaca. (See *Charters.*)
Marriage, the theory of, 52–3; political marriages and their effect, 58–66; political marriages of Cæsar, 59; of Pompey, 59–60; of Antony, 61–3; of Sextus Pompeius, 63–4.
Medicine, women and, 78–9; Soranus's advice to women physicians, 80–1; their specialties, 81–2; faith cures, 83; low social standing of physicians, 83.
Meetings, public, 105.
Municipal government, character of, 19; its decline, 19–20.
Municipal issues, 12–13.

N, the development of the letter, 256.
Nomination for office, 7, 19.
Novel, the Greek, 124–5.
Novel, the Roman, social conditions out of which it sprung, 117–9; literary conditions, 120; the Roman and Spanish novel, 125–6. (See also the *Satiræ.*)

O, the development of the letter, 253–4.
Octavia and Antony, 60–3; her struggle with Cleopatra, 61–3.

P, the development of the letter, 253–4.
Paleography, studied solely as an applied science, 234–6; its value as a pure science, 236–9; shows the working of evolutionary principles, 239; illustrated in development of Q, 240–253; of the other letters, 253–9.
Persius and his times, 131–3; his life and relations to Cornutus, 133–4; his Stoic training, 134–6; reason for writing satire, 136–7; con-

tempt for his art, 137–8; the poet and moralist, 138–9; his creed and that of the Puritans, 139–140; his relation to Horace and Cicero, 140–3; his dramatic power, 143–4.

Petrarch and the new learning, 145–7; his discovery of Cicero's "Letters," 147–8; his severe criticism of Cicero, 148–150; his later estimate, 152–5; his estimate of Virgil, 153–5.

Petronius and Sienkiewicz, 116; his death, 117. (See also the *Satiræ*.)

Plautus. (See the *Drama*.)

Poets, favorite Roman, 172–3.

Political posters, the appearance of, 4; their preparation, 8–9; addressed to individuals, 9–10; emanating from groups, 11, 14–17; ironical recommendations, 15–17; stereotyped formulæ, 18; rolls of honor, 20–1.

Pompeia. (See *Cæsar*.)

Pompeian wall paintings and classical stories, 181–3.

Pompey and Julia, 59–60.

Porcia and Brutus, 71–2.

Presidency, the, President Roosevelt's policy, 25–7; President Taft's policy, 27–8; the break in tenure of office, 32–3; held in check by the Senate, 34, 36–7.

Q, the development of the letter, 240–53.

R, the development of the letter, 257–8.

Restituta, the woman physician, 80.

Roselli, the epigraphical forger, 223–4.

S, the development of the letter, 253–4.

Salon, the, in politics, 55, 67. (See also *Marriage*.)

Salpensa. (See *Charters*.)

Satiræ, the, of Petronius, local color, 121–2; characters, 122; the Satiræ and women, 122; its motive, 123; development of plot, 124; its realism, 124, 126–9; an original product, 129–130; classical stories in the Satiræ, 179–181. (See also *Novel, the Roman*.)

Schools, Roman, 173–4.

Scribonia and Sextus Pompeius, 63–4.

Senate, the Roman, compared with Senate of the United States, 29–38; method of choosing senators, 29–30; experienced members, 30, 32–3; *esprit de corps* of senate, 30–1; conduct of business, 31; relation to consul, 32; continuity of policy, 33; confirms appointments, 34; may discredit administration, 35; exercises control over foreign affairs, 36–7; no limit on debate, 37–8; class prejudice, 39; inefficiency, 39.

Senate, the, of the United States, relations with the House, 24–5; with the President, 25–8, 32. (See also *Senate, the Roman*.)

Servilia, her antecedents, 66; her marriage to M. Junius

Brutus, 66; her relations with Cæsar, 67–70; she marries Silanus, 67; her democratic tendencies, 67; her course after Cæsar's death, 69–72; her influence with M. Brutus, 70–2.

Silvia. (See *Aetheria.*)

Society and politics, 64–6. (See also *Salon.*)

Soranus, 80–1.

Stoicism, the, of Persius, 134–6.

T, the development of the letter, 253–4.

Tanaquil, 44.

Terence. (See the *Drama.*)

Tertulla, 71.

Theatre, the, and women, 95–7; as a political factor, 106–114; political demonstrations in the theatre, 106–8; playwrights and contemporary politics, 108–111; actors and contemporary politics, 111–3; the mime and contemporary politics, 110–1. (See also *Drama.*)

Trades, women in the, 97–8.

Trigueros, the epigraphical forger, 226.

V, the development of the letter, 254.

Valerius's defence of women, 47.

Women, Roman, early ideal of womanhood, 41–2; women of the legendary period, 43–5; united political action of women, 45–53; individual women as political leaders, 53–76; women and the sumptuary laws, 45–8; women and taxation, 48–57; the "little senate" of women 50–1; the attitude of the Second Triumvirate toward women, 48–50; woman's acquisition of civil rights, 51–3; the theory of marriage, 52–3; woman's right to property, 52–3; women and the priesthoods, 78, 85–7; small number in the medical profession, 81; their medical specialties, 81–2; low social standing, 83; not allowed to be advocates, 84; their indirect influence on literature, 87; the diatribe of Juvenal, 87–8; slight literary productions of women, 89–90; Cornelia's Letters, 90–1; Sulpicia's poems, 91–2; Agrippina's Memoirs, 92–3; the Pilgrimage of Aetheria 93–5; women and the theatre, 95–7; women in the trades, 97–8; women in the brick business, 98. (See also *Marriage*, *Salon*, *Society*, and the names of women cited in this Index.)